BACKACHE AND DISC TROUBLES

Gives advice on locating the problem areas and sets out
a strategy for dealing with them. Also includes
guidelines on nutrition, lifestyle and the restoration of
strength and mobility.

THE NEW SELF HELP SERIES

BACKACHE AND DISC TROUBLES

A SELF-HELP STRATEGY FOR IDENTIFYING THE CAUSES OF YOUR BACKACHE AND SETTING ABOUT ELIMINATING THEM

ARTHUR WHITE
N.D., D.O.

Thorsons
An Imprint of HarperCollinsPublishers

Thorsons
An Imprint of HarperCollins*Publishers*
77–85 Fulham Palace Road,
Hammersmith, London W6 8JB.

Published by Thorsons 1989
5 7 9 10 8 6

© 1989 Thorsons Publishing Group

Arthur White asserts the moral right to
be identified as the author of this work

A catalogue record for this book is available
from the British Library

ISBN 0 7225 1935 4

Printed in Great Britain by
HarperCollins Manufacturing, Glasgow

Contents

Note to readers

Before following the self-help advice given in this book readers are earnestly urged to give careful consideration to the nature of their particular health problem, and to consult a competent physician if in any doubt. This book should not be regarded as a substitute for professional medical treatment, and whilst every care is taken to ensure the accuracy of the content, the author and the publishers cannot accept legal responsibility for any problem arising out of the experimentation with the methods described.

Introduction

A favourite axiom of the late Albert Rumfitt — for many years Dean and senior lecturer at the British College of Naturopathy and Osteopathy in London — was that the spine is the first part of the human anatomy to undergo the degenerative changes of the ageing process.

He could well have added that it is also the structure which causes more pain and disability than any other, for surveys in the United Kingdom have shown that, even in the first two decades of life, one person in every ten has already suffered some form of back pain, and the figure rises to close on 50 per cent for the population as a whole.

It is not surprising, therefore, that the cost to the community in the latter decades of the twentieth century had reached astronomical figures: close on £200 million a year is paid in sickness benefits for the loss of more than 30 million working days for which medical certificates of incapacity are issued, not to mention the additional short-term absenteeism by employees who do not consult a G.P.

To this vast sum must be added the one billion pounds incurred through lost productivity and nearly £160 million a year which is spent by the National Health Service for the treatment of back pain.

The consequences in terms of personal suffering and incapacity are no less serious, since more than ten per cent of the victims were found to have almost continuous pain, and in 50 per cent of these chronic cases it was necessary for the patient to seek a different occupation or take permanent retirement.

The situation appears to be even more serious in the U.S.A. where it was estimated that seven million people were receiving treatment for some form of back pain *on any one day*, and that 80 per cent of the population could expect to suffer backache at some time during life. Indeed, the research team suggested that this was an underestimation of the size of the problem and that the true figure should have been nearer 100 per cent!

As is the case in regard to many other common ailments the medical profession has little to offer those who seek relief from their suffering. Although anatomical and physiological research work has resolved many of the mysteries concerning the structural complexities of the human spine and the even more complex nervous system with which it is so intimately associated, the family doctor can usually do no more than sympathize with his patients and prescribe rest, warmth, and aspirin or one of the other analgesic drugs.

At best, these measures will afford some degree of relief from the often very severe pain which many patients experience, but at worst they do little or nothing to identify the causes of the backache and remedy them. Moreover, the prolonged use of pain-killing drugs is never without some degree of risk, because of the harmful side-effects to which all such medicines are known to give rise. Also, the relief of pain may lull the patient into a false sense of security and encourage him or her to return to work or indulge in physical activities which will reimpose harmful stresses on weakened muscles and supporting tissues and so cause a relapse or delay the healing processes.

It should be realized that pain is one of Nature's warning signals that something is amiss in the body and it is employed as a means of discouraging any activity which evokes or exacerbates the symptom.

By far the most common causes of back pain are excessive physical strain and injury caused by a jolt or unaccustomed movement. There is no pill or potion that a doctor or pharmacist can offer which will repair such damage or even hasten recovery, and it is for this reason that patients are turning increasingly to naturopaths and osteopaths for help and advice.

The purpose of this book is first to explain the basic mechanics of the human spine and its structures, secondly to outline the many factors which, singly or collectively, can weaken the back and render it suscep-tible to strain or injury, and then to describe the various naturopathic procedures which may be adopted to mobilize the body's very efficient self-healing and repair facilities.

Armed with this knowledge, the back-pain sufferer will not only be assured of obtaining the speediest possible relief, but he or she will also recognize that by one's own efforts it is possible to strengthen hitherto vulnerable tissues and so achieve a high degree of immunity from recurring bouts of painful disability.

1.

Back to the drawing-board

If we are to understand the significance of the various types and sites of back pain, and so appreciate the constructive purpose of naturopathic treatment measures, it is first essential to know something of the bony structures and the muscles, ligaments, and other tissues which enable us to move freely and carry out the extraordinary range of activities which, in health, we tend to take so much for granted.

Whether or not we accept the evolutionist theory that man is the culmination of millions of years of change and adaptation, the fact remains that he is the only creature who habitually maintains an erect posture. This unique characteristic undoubtedly affords many practical advantages, but it has to be accepted that it has also endowed us with certain structural weaknesses which have been accentuated by changes in our life-style and for which the present-day industrialized environment has been very largely responsible.

The mainstay of the human body is the spinal

column (see Figure 1, page 15) which consists of 33 bony segments resting one upon another. It serves as a strong but flexible central pillar which supports the head, and to which all the other movable bones — the ribs, shoulders, arms, pelvis, and legs — are firmly attached by tough ligaments.

A peculiarity of the spinal column is that its length — approximately 28 inches (70cm) — varies very little between one person and another, the overall height of the individual being mainly dependent upon the length of the lower limbs.

The bony segments which constitute the spinal column — the vertebrae — are all basically similar in general construction, although they have minor distinguishing features according to their location and the functions which they are required to serve.

Basically, each vertebra consists of a thick columnar section at the front — the body — behind which there is a ring of bone from which three spines protrude (see Figure 2, page 16). The bodies of the vertebrae form the main weight-bearing structure of the spine, hence those at the base of the column are substantially larger and stronger than those higher up the back.

The spines — one at the back of each vertebra and one on each side — provide attachment points for the ligaments and muscles which control the movements of the trunk and stabilize it in the erect position. With the vertebrae in position, one upon another, the bony rings form a continuous tube — the spinal canal — which houses and protects the spinal cord. The latter is the great nerve trunk by means of which sensory impulses from the organs of touch, pain, heat, cold,

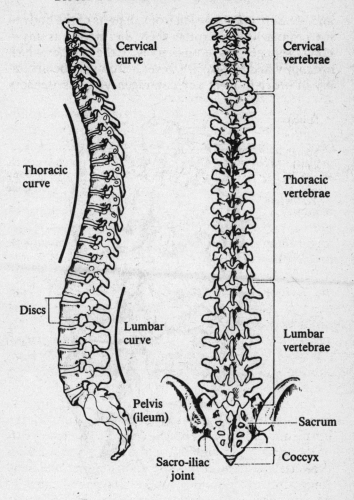

Figure 1: Side and rear views of the spinal column showing intervertebral discs and sacro-iliac joint.

and pressure are conveyed from all parts of the body to the brain which interprets them and transmits answering messages, via motor nerves, to the muscles which are motivated to take whatever action may be necessary in order to meet any contingency. Those sensory

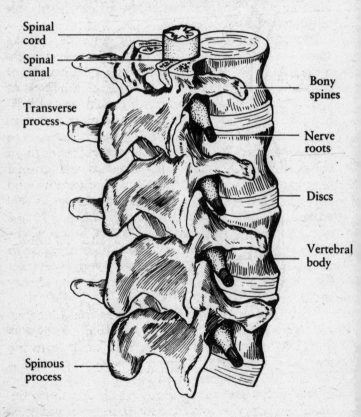

Spinal cord

Spinal canal

Transverse process

Bony spines

Nerve roots

Discs

Vertebral body

Spinous process

Figure 2: Spinal vertebrae showing discs and nerve roots emerging from spinal cord.

messages which pose a threat to our safety or survival are 'short-circuited' in the spinal cord in order to produce an instantaneous muscular response. The speed with which we withdraw a hand which comes into contact with excessive heat provides a graphic illustration of the extraordinary efficiency of this self-preservative mechanism.

In addition to the sensory and motor nerves, the spinal cord also houses an even more complex system of nerve fibres which are mainly independent of conscious control and which govern the functions of vital organs such as the heart, lungs, kidneys, glands, bladder, and liver. We cannot, for example, speed up or slow down the rate at which the heart continues to beat, night and day, throughout the 70 years or so which constitute what is regarded as the normal life-span. In a new-born baby the pulse-rate is around 130 beats per minute, and it decreases progressively until, in an adult, it stabilizes at approximately 70 in a man and 80 in a woman. During sleep, however, the pulse may fall as low as 40, whereas in response to vigorous exercise or a severe fright or other emotion the rate may double, returning to normal when activity ceases or the crisis is past.

These and many other involuntary vital functions are controlled by the brain through what is known as the autonomic nervous system, as distinct from the somatic system through which we exercise control of our bodily movements.

The millions of nerve fibres which constitute the spinal cord emerge from the base of the brain and enter the spinal canal which runs down the spinal column to the level of the second lumbar vertebra. On its way, it gives off a series of branches consisting of bundles of sensory and motor nerves which leave the spinal cord at intervals via apertures formed by notches in the bony rings of adjoining vertebrae (see Figure 2, page 16). The individual fibres then separate and ramify to adjacent areas — the motor fibres to the muscles and the sensory fibres to the minute end-organs which register pain, heat, cold, etc.

As will be explained in a later chapter, it is at the point where the nerve-roots emerge from the spine that they become vulnerable to injury, but in many cases such an eventuality becomes possible only as a result of degenerative changes which weaken and eventually impair the defensive mechanisms which operate so very efficiently in the healthy body.

We have already mentioned the near-circular apertures through which the nerve-branches pass when they leave the spinal cord and which are formed by the approximation of semi-circular notches above and below the adjacent pairs of vertebrae, the bodies of which are cushioned from each other by what are known as the intervertebral discs. These discs consist of an outer casing of very tough, fibrous cartilage enclosing an inner core of semi-fluid, pulpy material which has a high degree of elasticity.

This ingenious construction of the discs serves a double purpose. Firstly, it protects the spinal cord and the nerve-roots from injury by acting as a very efficient shock-absorber, and secondly it allows the spine to bend and twist. The extent to which these movements can be carried out varies in different parts of the spine, being greatest in the upper (cervical) and lower (lumbar) regions where the discs are thicker than in the central (thoracic) region where mobility is restricted by the rib-cage which is attached to the vertebrae.

Another important constructional feature of the human spine is that, instead of being straight like the mast of a ship, it is shaped like a flattened letter S when viewed from the side (see Figure 1, page 15). The two 'hollows' in the spine are necessary in order to accommodate the vital organs which are housed in the chest cavity, and the bowels, bladder, etc. in the abdomen. The forward curves in the neck and lumbar regions of the spine have developed during the evolutionary process to facilitate the maintenance of an erect posture. The curves also supplement the protective functions of the discs by imparting a degree of springiness to the spinal column and thus helping to absorb shocks due to falls and blows.

It needs little understanding of basic mechanics to appreciate that a column of so many small bones resting one upon another would be inherently unstable, even if it were perfectly straight and vertical. Inevitably, therefore, the degree of instability is increased enormously when a number of curves are built into the structure. Despite these apparant structural weaknesses, however, the human spine is capable not only of maintaining stability in the face of constantly changing postural demands but at the same time it can withstand and adjust to the often very considerable loads imposed upon it when we carry out tasks involving lifting, pulling, pushing, etc.

The innate stability of the human spine is achieved by connecting the individual vertebrae to each other by ligaments which are so tough that they are virtually indestructible. Indeed, when the healthy body is subjected to extreme violence as a result of falling from a great height, being struck by a car, or diving onto the head, it is more likely that the bony vertebrae will fracture than that the ligaments will be torn.

The mobility and strength of the spine are in turn dependent upon the elastic intervertebral discs, which we have mentioned previously, and upon a very complex network of muscles which are attached by strong tendons to the spines of the vertebrae and to anchorages on other skeletal components such as the shoulder-girdle, the pelvis, and the limbs.

The fact that so many people suffer various forms of backache is due not primarily to faulty design of the human spine and its complementary tissues and structures but to the abuses to which we, unwittingly perhaps, subject our bodies, or the degenerative changes which take place slowly and insidiously over the years due to ignorance or thoughtlessness. In many cases it is a combination of these and other factors which is responsible for most of the common back troubles, as I shall explain in a later chapter.

2.

Locating the problem areas

Backache is a term which may be used to describe a very considerable range of symptoms, from vague feelings of discomfort caused by tiredness or physical fatigue due to sitting or standing for a long period to the agonizing pain which results from a torn ligament or a disc lesion.

Between these extremes there are many other variations in both the severity of the symptoms and their location, not to mention the many factors which trigger off or relieve them and whether they are sporadic or continuous.

Although there are common causative factors which are implicated in many different forms of back trouble there are others which are remote from the area where the pain is experienced and it is important, therefore, that the true nature of the problem is determined in order that a safe and effective programme of self-treatment measures may be undertaken.

An extreme example is provided by a condition known as Pott's disease, or tuberculosis of the spine. In the early stages the symptoms — including backache — are vague and diffuse, but later there are serious degenerative changes in the bony tissues of the spine which cause crumbling of the vertebral bodies and increasing physical deformity and disability.

Cervical spondylitis is another potentially serious disease of the spine which is particularly troublesome in young adults. Its early stages are characterized by back pain and tenderness to touch over the affected areas due to inflammation of the soft tissues, and this may lead in time to bony outgrowths with fixation of the vertebral joints.

In older people, osteo-arthritis is a very common cause of back pain, and it has been estimated that the changes in the bony tissues which typify the disease are visible on X-ray examination in 90 per cent of individuals over the age of 40, although only a relatively small proportion complain of pain or other symptoms.

Degenerative conditions of this kind usually develop slowly over a very long period, and by the time the patient finds it necessary to seek professional advice it is likely that the symptoms, both local and generalized, will be sufficiently well established as to facilitate a reliable diagnosis.

For obvious reasons, therefore, any such condition must be excluded from consideration in a book of this nature, and we shall confine ourselves to the very much more common back problems such as the following, the nature and causes of which are likely to be readily identifiable.

General back pain
What is commonly known as fibrositis is likely to

afflict most of us at one time or another, regardless of age, but the term is a misnomer because inflammation of the fibrous tissues — e.g. tendons and ligaments — is relatively rare. Nowadays, it is customary to describe the condition as non-articular rheumatism, thus differentiating it from arthritis and the various other rheumatic disorders which affect the joints.

In its most common form it gives rise to a persistent, dull ache, typically affecting the area of the upper spine and shoulder-girdle, although it can be localized in almost any muscular tissue on the trunk and limbs. In some cases the onset is sudden, and the patient may experience considerable local pain and stiffness, particularly if a sudden movement is attempted or after a period of immobility, although the symptoms are usually relieved when the sufferer is asleep or resting, or when warmth is applied by a hot bath or the application of a hot-water bottle.

In severe cases there may be areas of acute tenderness when pressure is applied, and it may be possible to feel hard nodules at these points due to localized spasm of the muscle fibres.

Neck pain and stiffness

The most frequent causes of pain and stiffness in the upper spine are nervous tension and the gradual build-up of fibrous tissue in the muscles due to inactivity. For many people, nowadays, sedentary and other occupational factors tend to reduce the degree of mobility in the vertebral joints of the neck. For example, when working at a desk or bench, or when reading, watching television, driving a car, or taking part in many other occupational or passive recreational activities it is only very rarely that the head needs to be turned more than a few degrees in either direction, and for long periods the muscles which support and balance its not inconsiderable weight remain locked in a state of passive tension.

Inevitably, therefore, their normally elastic tissues become increasingly thickened and fibrous and so liable to strain and possible injury when circumstances impose a need for any unaccustomed degree of rotation, flexion, or extension.

Thoracic pain

Faulty posture is a very common cause of pain in the thoracic spine — the twelve vertebrae to which the ribs are attached — as it is in other areas, particularly in children and adolescents in whom rapid growth and physical development are taking place.

Teenagers are often very self-conscious about their height and other physical characteristics which differ in any way from what is considered to be 'normal' and which tend to invite what is often quite devastating ridicule from others in their age-group. Consequently, a subconscious desire to conceal the 'abnormality' may cause them to adopt a head-down, round-shouldered posture which if maintained for a year or two, can create a postural anomaly that is hard to correct in later life. The problem may be further compounded because, at that juncture in his or her life, the child is likely to spend many hours bent over school books at a low desk. This type of postural defect — an excessive forward curve of the upper spine — is termed a kyphosis.

Another variant of the same problem is termed

scoliosis. It takes the form of a marked lateral curvature of the thoracic spine which is often compensated by a similar curve of the lower — lumbar — spine in the opposite direction. In young people it can be induced by habitually sitting askew at a desk supported on one elbow, standing frequently with the weight on one foot, sitting with one leg crossed over the other, or regularly carrying a heavy burden on one arm or shoulder. The latter practice is a frequent cause of backache in young mothers who, for many months, may carry an increasingly heavy child for quite long periods every day.

An excessive kyphotic curve is a common concomitant of the ageing process due to progressive weakening of the supporting muscles and ligaments and shrinkage of the intervertebral discs — a process which explains the progressive decrease in body height which is apparent in many older people.

Low back pain

The lumbar vertebrae at the base of the spine are subjected to enormous stresses in the course of normal physical activities because in addition to their role in supporting the major part of the body-weight they are also subjected to considerable flexion, extension, and torsional stresses when we bend, straighten, and turn, while at the same time lifting or carrying loads which may weigh in excess of 50kg (1 cwt).

Not surprisingly, therefore, what is termed 'lumbago' is one of the most frequent and painful physical afflictions from which so many people suffer at one time or another during their working lives. It is characterized by a sudden seizure in the lower back accompanied by a very acute stabbing pain, the onset of which almost invariably occurs during the process of lifting a heavy object or performing some unaccustomed strenuous work or exercise. The pain is aggravated by any sudden movement, and the resultant protective spasm of the muscles may cause the back and thighs to 'lock' in the flexed position, so that it is temporarily impossible for the erect position to be regained.

Similarly, the pain may be exacerbated when attempting to rise from a chair, or by coughing or sneezing, or even drawing a deep breath.

Sciatica

This very common afflication causes severe pain along the course of the great sciatic nerve which emerges from the spinal cord at the base of the spine, passes through the buttocks and traverses the thigh and leg into the foot. In addition to pain which may be experienced at any point served by the nerve, or along its entire length, the patient may also suffer sensory anomalies — e.g. numbness, 'pins and needles' sensations, or a feeling of abnormal warmth confined to the affected areas.

The symptoms are the result of inflammation of the nerve or to compression of the nerve-root at the point where it issues from between the lumbar vertebrae, and in most cases only one limb is affected.

Sacro-iliac strain

The sacro-iliac joint is situated at the base of the spine where the triangular sacrum slots into the v-shaped space between the two 'wings' of the pelvic girdle (see Figure 1, page 15). Great strength is required of this joint because it is the fulcrum through which very considerable forces are transmitted in the process of bending down and lifting heavy weights, but the ingenious design of the joint ensures maximum strength while permitting a slight degree of movement between the adjoining surfaces. The slight 'springing' effect which this arrangement imparts to the joint serves not only to cushion any shocks imposed at this point but, in the case of women, it allows the pelvic girdle to widen at the end of pregnancy and thus facilitate the birth of the baby.

Because of the resulting greater mobility of the female joint women are more susceptible than men to the slight displacement which is termed sacro-iliac strain, particularly in the weeks following childbirth when the supporting ligaments are still relaxed.

This lesion, which is one of the most common with which osteopaths are called upon to deal, is characterized by a dull aching pain and a feeling of discomfort, particularly after having being seated for some time.

The pain, which is usually intermittent at first but gradually becomes more persistent, spreads from the buttocks down the leg, often following the course of the sciatic nerve, and it is accentuated when the thigh is flexed on the abdomen with the knee fully extended.

Disc lesions

What is variously termed slipped disc, prolapsed disc or herniated disc is a relatively rare but potentially serious condition which usually results in a sudden, immobilizing pain in the lower back and a progressive extension of the symptom into the buttocks and down the length of the leg.

More rarely, a disc between the lower cervical vertebrae may be damaged, in which case the pain and other symptoms will extend into the shoulder-blade and down the arm.

Although degenerative changes in the supporting tissues of the spine and the disc itself, due to poor health or ageing, may be contributory factors, this type of lesion is by no means uncommon in young people who are physically strong and athletically active. In these cases, damage to the disc usually results from a fall, or a severe strain or some similar injury.

In the early stages, the pain will be so severe that the patient will be incapable of extending the affected limb, and will be compelled to sit with the leg drawn up in order to obtain some degree of relief. He will only be able to move, if at all, with the body doubled over at the hips, or he may even be reduced to crawling on hands and knees.

At this stage, also, it may be impossible for the sufferer to lie down and so he may find it necessary to sleep in an armchair or propped up on a couch.

In response to the pain, the muscles on the affected side of the body may go into spasm in order to prevent movement, and as a result a lateral curvature of the spine away from the lesion may be clearly apparent.

The pain will usually begin to abate during the course of a few days, but some degree of disability will in most cases persist for a period of from six to eight weeks. During this time, however, other symptoms may become manifest, depending on the extent and site of the disc lesion. They may include loss of sensory response to pain, heat, and cold in certain areas of the thigh, leg and foot, and in the case of severe injury there may be wasting of some of the muscles in these areas with consequent weakness.

Although, for the sake of convenience and clarity, we have separated the various types of backache into localized categories, it must be appreciated that, because of the structural features of the spine, any strain, injury, or defect which causes problems in one specific area is likely to give rise to other but probably less obvious symptoms in other regions.

For example, sciatic pain extending down the left leg is likely to cause the sufferer to walk with a limp and transfer most of his or her body weight to the right leg in order to take pressure off the affected limb. As a result, the left hip will be lowered, inducing a lateral curvature of the lumbar spine with its concavity to the right. In order to compensate for the resulting imbalance another curve is likely to develop in the thoracic spine with its concavity to the left. These adjustments will impose unaccustomed strain on muscles and ligaments in the upper spine so that secondary pain and stiffness are likely to be experienced eventually in these areas.

This is a factor which needs to be borne in mind when, in a later chapter, we consider what needs to be done firstly to relieve the primary symptoms as quickly as possible and secondly to strengthen the muscles, tendons, and ligaments which balance and support the spine and to identify and eliminate the causes of the original back problem.

It is to the latter factors that we shall now turn our attention.

3.

Predisposing factors — faulty nutrition

Some types of backache have a very sudden and dramatic onset, whereas many more of these problems develop slowly and either persist or worsen or recur sporadically with varying degrees of severity.

It is true to say, however, that in virtually all back troubles there are a number of preconditioning — or more correctly *de*conditioning — factors which have weakened the soft tissues of the spine, and possibly other parts of the body, and caused them to break down when subjected to an unusual degree of stress.

A really healthy body, maintained in good physical condition, should have such a wide margin of tolerance in all its tissues — bone, muscle, ligaments, tendons, etc. — that it should be virtually impossible to overtax its resources through the performance of any normal activity. Tendons and ligaments should be sufficiently tough as to be able to withstand any strain that the muscles are capable of imposing on them, whether it be the result of lifting, pulling, pushing, bending, or turning, or any other normal activity with which the body is required to cope.

This means that tissue breakdown and injury could occur only as a result of the body being subjected to an abnormal stress such as that resulting from a fall, a severe blow, a heavy jolt, the sudden imposition of an unexpectedly heavy burden, or some other traumatic eventuality. Unfortunately, under modern living conditions, very few people — including even highly trained athletes — are able to attain and maintain such a degree of physical perfection, and there are many factors which, often without our knowledge, slowly and insidiously undermine our general health and lower the tone and resilience of the complex tissues which enable us to carry out the many diverse and often demanding activities which we tend to take for granted. Until, that is, as a result of a moment's thoughtlessness, or carelessness, or over-enthusiasm we demand too much of our bodies and a muscle, or tendon, or ligament or even a bone gives way under the strain.

Strangely enough, what are undoubtedly the two most important factors in maintaining the complex cells of which our vital tissues are constructed — namely, the food we eat and the beverages we drink — are perhaps the most widely misunderstood and neglected. It is true that diet and nutrition are the subject of increasing attention in the newspapers, magazines, and radio and television programmes, but unfortunately much of the information thus disseminated is put out by professional public relations organizations on behalf of various commercial elements in the food industry. As a result, the claims and counterclaims of the various vested interests which are competing for a larger share of the enormous public expenditure on food and drink leave the housewife baffled and bewildered and unable to assess the nutritional properties of the vast range of colourfully packaged products which line the supermarket shelves.

We have only to stand for a short time at the check-out point of such an establishment to realize that most of the trolleys are piled high with tins and packets which, if we could study the labels, contain a conglomeration of processed and denatured products laced with a hotch-potch of chemical preservatives, colourings, flavourings, extenders, etc., the multi-syllabic names or abstruse numerical designations of which are likely to be totally meaningless to anyone but an industrial chemist.

For a further insight into the feeding habits of a large section of the public let us now stroll a little further down the High Street and see what is on offer in the ubiquitous 'take-away' cafés, fast-food restaurants, and 'burger' establishments. Whatever the time of day, the tables are likely to be crowded with mainly young patrons indulging in such popular delicacies as fried fish, sausages, hamburgers, beefburgers, pizzas, etc., with chips or white bread, liberally sprinkled with condiments and colourful sauces, and washed down with cola drinks, tea, or coffee.

These, then, are the raw materials with which the consumer's body is expected to perform the near miracle of constructing and maintaining skin, flesh, bone, hair, nerves, blood, and other specialized tissues as well as the glands and their complex chemical secretions which keep our vital organs — the heart, lungs, liver, brain, kidneys, etc., — functioning efficiently, day after day and year after year throughout life.

Admittedly, many schools nowadays devote a part of the curriculum to such subjects as biology and nutrition, but few teachers have more than a very basic knowledge of these subjects and so they must of necessity rely on orthodox text-books for most of the information which they disseminate. The result is that children are given to understand that in order for the human body to grow and function efficiently it is only necessary to provide it with a daily quota of calories, and so many grams of protein and fat, and varying amounts of the more specialized nutrients such as vitamins and minerals.

It is almost exclusively a *quantitative* evaluation, with virtually no consideration of *qualitative* factors. Consequently, the abiding impression that is implanted in young minds is that starchy, sugary, and fatty foods are good sources of heat and energy, that meat is the best source of body-building protein, and that if you don't like vegetables, salads, or fruit you can obtain all the vitamins you need in a packet or bottle at the chemist's shop.

Adults, too, are encouraged to accept similar nutritional yardsticks by the slogans and half-truths which are dreamed up by the highly professional copy-writers employed by advertising agencies who are paid millions of pounds annually by the giants of the food industry for their services in convincing the public not only that a silk purse *can* be made from a sow's ear, but that the latter is vastly superior to the genuine product.

Complex laws and regulations have been devised to outlaw the more blatant falsehoods and inaccuracies which were an all too common feature of advertising in the past, but these efforts have been largely aborted by the skilful use of words and pictures which promise by implication something which may not be claimed directly.

Ambiguity is the name of the game, and millions of people are deceived into thinking that cooked and processed concoctions of denatured food materials which have been artificially flavoured, coloured, preserved, and laced with other products of the chemical laboratory are in fact a nutritionally equal or even superior substitute for a wholesome staple food.

There is probably no better example of the way in which a food product is processed and manipulated for commercial purposes than that provided by our daily bread. For more than a century the white loaf has virtually monopolized the bread markets of the Western world, and until quite recently the nutritional experts have almost unanimously insisted that those who claimed that wholemeal bread was fundamentally superior were at best harmless cranks and at worst charlatans.

The orthodox nutritional text-books contained tables which appeared to demonstrate quite clearly that analyses of white and wholemeal loaves showed virtually no differences in regard to the respective calorific values and the amounts of the more important nutrients — e.g. iron, calcium, and protein — which they contained. On a purely *quantitative* basis such claims could not be challenged, but it was in terms of the nature and *quality* of the nutrients that the 'food cranks' denounced the white loaf as a major health hazard.

Wholemeal bread, they maintained, was made from flour milled from the whole wheat-grain in which nutrients such as iron and calcium were incorporated in their natural form and in balanced proportions. In the milling processes which are used to produce refined white flour, however, the outer layers of the wheat are sifted out, and with them are extracted the wheat germ and a major proportion of the mineral content. Having been convinced — albeit reluctantly — that the consequential loss of calcium and iron from a staple food could have a damaging effect on the health of the consumer, the authorities decreed that all flour, other than 100 per cent wholemeal, must be 'fortified' by the addition of synthetic iron and *creta preparata*, which is the euphemistic name for common chalk.

It was not until several decades later that it dawned on the nutritional 'experts' that the removal of bran from the flour during the refining process was largely responsible for a number of bowel disorders, including constipation, colitis, and diverticulitis. Hitherto, they maintained that bran was an inert substance which had no nutritional or physiological value and, indeed, it was common practive for doctors to advise patients suffering from bowel disorders to have an exclusively 'bland' diet — i.e. the very foods which it was now recognized were the major cause of their problems.

The 'diet cranks', who had proclaimed the virtues of wholemeal bread and other natural foods, were thus vindicated once again.

The reader may well be wondering what all this talk about foods and nutrition has to do with the subject of back pain. The answer is simple: if, as we have already suggested, a major contributory cause of back troubles is structural weakness of the tendons and ligaments which are called upon to support the spine, it is surely self-evident that if these problems are to be solved the damaged tissues need to be repaired and strengthened.

This, in turn, implies that we must provide the body with the building materials which it needs in order to replace weak and damaged cells with new, healthy tissue. The 'silk purse' metaphor is just as relevant to the human body as it is to all the items of equipment which we use constantly in our daily lives. Whether it be a car, or furniture, a washing-machine, or any other piece of domestic apparatus, it is universally recognized that its efficiency and reliability are dependent to a very large extent on the quality of the materials used in its construction. Unfortunately, throughout the twentieth century there has been an increasing trend towards the use of cheap and inferior materials in the mass-production of all these goods, except the most expensive and exclusive items, on the basis that when, as happens inevitably sooner rather than later, it disintegrates or ceases to function, the owner will discard it and purchase a replacement.

It is a commercial philosophy which bodes ill for the future of the antique dealers, for it is unlikely that many of today's artefacts will survive to become collector's items in the twenty-first century!

The human body cannot be so casually discarded and replaced, however, and even the most skilful achievements of the transplant surgeons are unlikely to do more than patch up a failing body and postpone for a few years the inevitable final disintegration.

Clearly, then, it behoves us to look realistically at the health problems and disabilities that beset us from time to time, identify the causes and take rational steps to correct them if we are to stave off the worst degenerative effects of the ageing process. In pursuit of this very desirable goal the first priority must be to ensure that the fuel which stokes our vital fires and the materials which we use for the growth, repair, and maintenance of our bodies are of the highest biological quality. This should be our *only* criteria when we select the food we eat, the fluids we drink, and even the air we breathe. The latter, of course, is something over which we have little direct control, except insofar as tobacco-smoking is concerned, but we can and should be intelligently selective when it comes to choosing what foods and beverages we purchase and consume.

If you fear that such an injunction presages a lengthy dissertation on such dietetic intangibles as vitamins, minerals, calories, trace elements, etc., I hasten to reassure you that such minutae lie in the province of the laboratory and the analytical chemists whose main ambition in life appears to be to discover more and more about less and less, regardless of whether the results of their experiments are likely to be of any practical value to anyone except perhaps another analytical chemist who, in all probability, will challenge their validity.

History provides ample proof that today's 'experts' are tomorrow's joke-fodder, whether it be in the area of nutrition, medicine, or any other field of natural science. The simple fact is that the human body and its metabolic processes are so extraordinarily complex and variable that no one has as yet been able to assess with any degree of certainty the quantities of any nutrient that are needed to guarantee systemic health and functional efficiency.

Scarcely a week passes without the appearance in a newspaper or magazine, or on a radio or telelvision programme, of a report by a so-called 'expert' to the effect that such-and-such a food or drink has been found to contain a substance which causes such-and-such a symptom of disease. Rarely, in such reports, are any details given of the nature of the experiments which led to these revolutionary and potentially frightening discoveries, and even more rarely do we hear of any subsequent repercussions.

The reasons are quite simple: every natural commodity which we consume is made up of a complex amalgam of substances in precisely metered quantities which, during growth and development, are brought together and combined in such a way as to form a unique whole, designed by Nature to serve as a wholesome food. The human metabolic system is likewise uniquely designed to take the things we eat, separate them into their various components, subject them to a vastly complex series of chemical processes and then either assimilate what is needed for growth and maintenance at that particular time, or neutralize any potentially harmful substances and excrete unwanted residues.

The scientist, using highly sophisticated equipment and techniques, takes the raw food materials, separates and concentrates their various components, and then either feeds them to, or injects them into, a laboratory animal such as a rat, a monkey or a guinea-pig. It is hardly surprising that many of the unfortunate recipients should develop a systemic disorder or organic defect, because not only does it receive a massive concentration of a substance which, in nature, would be consumed only in minute quantities and in combination with other nutritional components, but the food product from which the concentrate is derived may well be one with which its digestive chemical processes are totally unfamiliar and therefore unable to assimilate.

Again, our daily bread provides an excellent example of the way in which the results of scientific research can mislead the most knowledgeable experts. In 1925 a noted nutritionist, Sir Edward Mellanby, carried out experiments on puppies who were given a diet which was deficient in vitamin D and calcium but which contained large quantities of bread. He found that the puppies which ate the most bread grew at the fastest rate but also developed the severest rickets. Moreover, it was noted that the bone deformities were worse in those dogs fed on wholewheat bread than in those given white bread. Subsequent research led to the conclusion that there is a substance called phytic acid which is present in the wholewheat bread which interferes with the absorption of calcium, the implication being that white bread is superior to wholewheat as a source of dietary calcium. Even today that claim is still put forward in some quarters, despite the fact that it has long been realized that many cereals, including wheat, contain an enzyme called phytase which is capable of neutralizing the effects of phytic acid and so facilitating the absorption of calcium.

An interesting by-product of this research was the realization that although oats contain phytic acid their phytase content is low, and it was assumed at first that this was the reason why puppies fed on this cereal were especially liable to develop rickets. But researchers were faced with the puzzling anomaly that although puppies fed on oats developed rickets, the porridge-eating Scots appeared to be singularly immune to the disease. So how could this be explained? The answer, apparently, is quite simple: the digestive system of those who habitually eat oats or any other cereal has developed the ability to neutralize phytic acid and so assimilate calcium efficiently, whereas a puppy, which is a carnivorous animal and does not normally eat cereals, has no such metabolic facility.

This is but one example of the type of short-sighted 'expert' research which has bedevilled the subject of nutrition for many decades and which will no doubt continue to do so. It behoves us, therefore, to maintain a healthy scepticism in regard to the often alarming and confusing pronouncements of the 'fragmentary nutritionists'. The guiding principle which naturo-paths have always propounded is that we should rely as far as possible on simple, whole foods, eaten preferably in their original unprocessed form, which will supply all the essential nutrients — proteins, fats, carbohydrates, vitamins, minerals, and roughage — in their natural proportions and combinations and with the minimum risk of contamination with potentially harmful chemicals in the form of flavourings, condi-tioners, colourings, preservatives, extenders, etc. which should have no place in human nutrition.

We maintain that faulty nutrition is a major causa-tive factor in many of the illnesses which afflict civilized man and which are largely responsible for the progressive tissue degeneration and eventual breakdown which result in disabling diseases and injuries such as back pain and arthritis.

This is the simple message to all health-seekers to which I shall return in greater detail in a later chapter.

4.

Predisposing factors — structural weakness

If denatured food and nutritional deficiencies and excesses are public health enemy number one then the erosion of physical fitness resulting from so-called improvements in our living standards must surely qualify as a very close runner-up.

Well within the memory of many people still living today, walking was by far the most widely used form of transport for distances of two or three miles or more, and the bicycle then took over for longer journeys of anything up to, and often exceeding, 100 miles. Public transport was only resorted to when speed or convenience were primary considerations, and even then a walk was entailed in order to reach a bus or tram route or a railway station.

All this has changed since the middle years of the twentieth century, thanks to the massive increase in car ownership as a result of which many people no longer walk even a few hundred yards to a shop or station, or to visit friends or a place of entertainment. From their earliest days children are taken to and from school by car or bus, and the family car is usually available at week-ends whenever transport is needed for leisure activities.

At home, it is the television set which has still further eroded the need for physical activity, and even the long summer evenings are often spent sprawled in a comfortable chair in front of 'the box' without even the need to do more than flick a switch to change from one programme to another.

It is an immutable law of Nature that what we do not use we lose, and it is inevitable therefore that the price we pay for leading a largely sedentary and inactive life is the gradual loss of muscle-tone and a weakening of tendons and ligaments. Anyone who, through illness or injury, has been confined to bed for even two or three weeks will have experienced the very considerable loss of strength resulting from the rapid wasting of unused muscle tissue, and the equally speedy restoration of physical capacity which comes with the return of mobility. What many people do not appreciate, however, is that the effects of inactivity are not confined to joints and muscles but ramify throughout the entire system, for the simple reason that without regular vigorous exercise the circulatory system cannot function efficiently and so the cells of the vital organs and other tissues are starved of the nutrients which are transported to them via the bloodstream.

Most of us are aware that the heart is a muscular pump which works continuously to distribute blood to all parts of the body via the arteries, but that is only part of the circulatory process. Once the blood reaches the tissues to which it is directed it passes through a network of minute capillaries, at which point oxygen and essential nutrients are taken up by the cells in exchange for carbon-dioxide and waste materials. The blood then enters the veins through which it completes its circulatory tour of duty, but by this time the propulsive effect of the heart has been almost completely dissipated and so other mechanisms have to be brought into play to propel the vital fluid upward from the lower limbs and abdomen against the not inconsiderable force of gravity.

To achieve this, Nature has harnessed what has been aptly described as the 'muscle pump' — i.e. utilizing the contraction and relaxation of the muscles of the lower limbs during exercise in order to compress the large veins which are channelled between them, and thus forcing the blood upward into the abdomen. A series of valves at strategic points in the veins prevents the reflux of the blood when the muscles relax.

Another effect of strenuous exercise is to create a need for oxygen, with the result that breathing becomes deeper and faster. This in turn causes the muscular diaphragm which separates the chest from the abdomen to rise and fall more vigorously, thus augmenting the effects of the 'muscle-pump' by sucking and forcing the blood through the large veins which pass upward through the abdomen and into the chest cavity where they return the spent blood to the heart.

It will be appreciated, therefore, why inactivity and a sedentary mode of life will have such far-reaching effects, since without the aid of the 'muscle-pump' there is a pooling of blood in the abdomen and lower limbs, starving all the tissues of nutrients and causing an accumulation of carbon-dioxide and waste products.

The human organism has a very considerable capacity to withstand abuse and misuse, but when these are sustained for long periods it is inevitable that tissues and organs will begin to degenerate and eventually break down. Among the more obvious effects of inactivity are varicose veins, haemorrhoids, and abdominal weakness and distension, but far more insidious is the deterioration which takes place in the cellular structure of the deeper tissues and organs — including the cartilages, muscles, and tendons of the spinal column which are called upon to withstand the recurring and often excessive demands which are imposed upon them during the course of our daily duties.

There is, perhaps, no better example of the insidious effects of habitual inactivity than the deterioration which takes place in the heart itself and which is now widely recognized as being largely responsible for the alarming increase in coronary heart disease among the population as a whole and particularly middle-aged men. The heart, as we have already explained, is basically a muscular pump consisting of four interconnecting chambers which contract and relax rhythmically to provide the initial impetus which propels the blood through the arterial system to every organ and tissue of the body. In a healthy individual, at rest, electrical impulses from the brain maintain a regular pulse-rate averaging 70 beats per minute, although this can vary quite widely, particularly in the case of trained athletes in whom pulse-rates as low as 40 may be recorded when at rest.

The explanation for this phenomenon is that the

strenuous training routines to which athletes subject themselves strengthen and enlarge the heart so that a greater volume of blood is circulated with each beat. These, however, are relatively rare exceptions today, and if we look at the other side of the coin it will be found that in those who lead a sedentary life the heart becomes progressively smaller and weaker and the pulse-rate increases in order to maintain an adequate degree of circulatory efficiency. If, however, there is any increase in the work-load on such a heart it will not have the reserve capacity or muscular strength with which to respond to the demand for extra oxygen. Sudden exertion, such as is entailed in running for a bus or train, or climbing a flight of stairs, may well overtax the limited resources of the heart and cause a catastrophic failure. An outburst of temper can have equally serious results, because the release of adrenalin into the bloodstream which is triggered off by any such emotional crisis will stimulate the heart into increased action to which it may be unable to respond. Even relatively light exercise taken immediately following a large meal may have disastrous consequences for someone who is overweight and out of condition.

This brief digression from our main subject is necessary in order to underline the naturopathic concept that weakness or failure in any one type of tissue or organ is almost invariably indicative of impending problems elsewhere in the body. That is why treatment measures which are necessary to repair or strengthen a weakened back must of necessity be designed to provide the means and materials which will restore the body's ability to rebuild damaged tissues and restore to normal the functional capacity of all its organs.

The spinal discs are no less dependent upon regular maintenance than the heart and other body tissues. Just as physical exercise is necessary to activate the 'muscle-pump' and propel a nutrient-laden blood-supply to all parts of the body, so the alternate flexion and extension of the spinal column during the course of physical activity compresses and decompresses the discs, sucking in nutrients and forcing out waste materials.

It cannot be stressed too strongly that it is incumbent upon each individual to mobilize for himself or herself the body's tremendous capacity for self-repair and self-healing. No one, however skilled, can *cure* our ailments or repair our injuries. At best a practitioner, of any school of healing, can only identify the causes of our problems and advise us what needs to be done to mobilize our self-healing resources. At worst, he may prescribe a drug or carry out an operation which may relieve a pain or other symptom for a time or remove or replace a defective organ, but because such methods do nothing to remedy the causes of the problem a weakened body will inevitably deteriorate further.

Most people readily accept the fact that when a bone is broken or flesh is torn, the damage will be repaired and the injured tissues will heal with no external intervention other than that which is necessary to cleanse the wound, ease the pain and ensure rest and warmth for the sufferer. No medicine or pill can hasten recovery. We simply take it for granted that the body will mobilize whatever resources are needed to seal off ruptured blood-vessels, cover an open wound with a protective scab and then, cell by cell, reconstruct the damaged tissue with remarkable speed and efficiency.

The naturopathic approach to back problems, therefore, is firstly to ensure that the material needed for repair and reconstruction of damaged tissues are of the best quality and that they are provided in the correct quantities and combinations and, secondly, to brief the patient fully as to what he or she needs to do, or refrain from doing, in order to allow the body's self-healing mechanisms to carry out their functions as speedily and efficiently as possible.

Having explained at some length what are undoubtedly the two most important predisposing causes of back troubles — i.e. faulty nutrition and structural weakness — I shall conclude my summary of causative factors by explaining the contributory role that is played by faulty posture, obesity, and stress in the eventual breakdown of the tissues and structures on which we rely so heavily throughout our lives.

5.

Stress and tension

In my description of the spinal column in an earlier chapter I explained the structural significance of the series of four curves which are a feature of the human back-bone.

Because the strength and stability of this complex structure are dependent on the manner and extent to which these curves compensate for each other it should be readily understood that any appreciable deviation from the normal will inevitably be detrimental to the functional efficiency not only of the spine itself but of the other tissues, structures, and organs which it supports.

Consequently, when the tendons and ligaments become weakened as a result of poor nutrition and lack of exercise, there is a tendency for the curves to increase insidiously with the passage of time, and in some cases abnormal lateral curves will be superimposed on the natural fore-and-aft ones.

By far the most common postural defect is the result of an exaggeration of both the thoracic and lumbar curves (see Figure 1, page 15) as a result of which the shoulders become rounded and the abdomen is thrust forward and downward — a defect which is seen frequently in desk-workers, draughtsmen, and those whose occupation entails long periods of standing.

The by-products of these postural abnormalities are many. Starting with the upper spine, the accentuated thoracic curve produces a compensatory backward kink in the neck as a result of which nerves and blood-vessels may be compressed, which in turn can give rise to sporadic headaches and bouts of dizziness. It may also be a contributory factor in some cases of migraine and head-noises.

Another result of the accentuated thoracic curve is that the chest is cramped and this constricts the movement of the ribs. As a result, lung capacity is reduced, the blood is deprived of oxygen, and carbon-dioxide accumulates, resulting in premature tiredness and lethargy.

Finally, the forward thrust of the lumbar spine allows the abdomen to sag, thus imposing abnormal pressure on the organs which it houses. As a result, bowel function may become sluggish and the bladder may be compressed. In men, this may lead in time to prostate congestion and urinary troubles, while in women it can affect the ovaries and uterus, resulting in certain menstrual disorders.

All of these problems are, of course, in addition to the various types of backache which are our main concern. They need to be mentioned, however, in order that readers may be fully appreciative of the naturopathic principle that *all* bodily structures and organs are interdependent one upon another, and that dysfunction in any one area will almost inevitably cause problems elsewhere.

Similarly, no single factor can ever be held responsible for any bodily defect, and we need to be aware of the many ways in which seemingly innocuous everyday habits and practices can combine to cause physical defects or systemic malfunction.

Thus, while occupational factors may play a major part in the development of postural defects and the various disabilities with which they in turn may be associated, the 'hidden extras' which may play a supporting role can include design faults in such diverse items as footwear, beds, chairs, and car seats.

Despite repeated warnings, young women in particular persist in wearing shoes the design of which could hardly be more potentially harmful. High heels, pointed toes, and sling backs have been a feature of fashionable feminine footwear for decades, and it is a tribute to the tolerance and adaptability of the human body that these atrocities can be inflicted on it without causing more obvious deformities and disabilities.

The fact that women constitute a very large proportion of those who seek treatment from chiropodists is but one consequence of their obsession with appearances at the expense of their physical welfare, but far more damaging are the postural defects which develop insidiously as a result of the inbuilt instability and strain to which they subject themselves.

The need to walk constantly on tip-toe and to maintain balance on a high heel — one version of which is aptly terms a 'stiletto' — keeps the muscles of the calves and thighs constantly in tension and forces the knees forward; this in turn causes the pelvis

to tilt forward, increasing the hollow lumbar curve
and necessitating a compensatory increase in the thoracic curve.

We have seen already that an efficient circulation,
on which cell nutrition and bodily health are so heavily
dependent, can only be maintained with the aid of the
'muscle-pump' action provided by physical activity,
and it will be realized, therefore, that if the muscles of
the legs and thighs are kept in a state of tension for
lengthy periods this essential circulatory boost will not
be able to operate efficiently.

Chair design is another area in which fashion
considerations frequently take precedence over bodily
comfort and physical welfare. Indeed, it would appear
that the principle aim of those responsible for some of
the trendier furniture is to produce a settee or what is
euphemistically termed an 'easy chair' which ignores
even the most basic anatomical considerations. Low-
slung seats which are almost grotesquely deep from
front to back leave the occupant sprawled amost at
floor level but with the front edge of the cushion
propping his or her legs at mid-calf level so that the feet
are suspended above the floor. By contrast, the back
cushion is cut so low that only the shoulder-blades are
supported, ensuring that the neck muscles must be
maintained in a state of constant tension in order to
support the head.

It appears to be the more fashion-conscious younger
people who tend to be attracted by this type of
furniture, preferring to follow the design dictates of the
glossy magazines and presumably indifferent to any
considerations of comfort or postural shortcomings.

Older people, it has been observed, show more

regard for the practical aspects of furniture design and are likely to select a firmer, higher, and more straight-backed chair which provides adequate support for the thighs, back, and head and from which they can rise with the minimum effort and strain on knees and hips.

They are, however, more likely to persist in sleeping in a bed or on a mattress the springs of which have become weakened from years of use and which, as a result, sag to such an extent that the spine is subjected to distortion and lateral strain.

Distortion of the upper spine can frequently be traced to the type of pillow used to support the head. A pillow that is too high or too low will impose a sustained lateral flexion on the neck in the side-lying position, and a high pillow will flex the neck forward when lying on the back.

The increasing trend towards reliance on the motor-car as a means of daily transport is another potentially damaging factor where the human spine is concerned, for although the vehicle manufacturers have undoubt-edly made considerable strides in terms of seat design, they are hampered by the fact that the men and women for whom they have to cater differ very substantially in regard to such physical characteristics as height, leg-length, and weight. Moreover, with the exception of a few luxury models, the space into which the seats and the passengers have to be packed is very restricted, and these limiting factors dictate that ideals must be subordinated in favour of practicalities. Even the best design, therefore, must be a computerized com-promise based on the physical characteristics of a mythical 'average' human being, with the result that the seating arrangements of the vast majority of cars are likely to present shortcomings for all but a very small proportion of drivers, particularly those who are required to spend many hours at the wheel during the course of their occupational commitments.

Obesity is another factor which has become increasingly significant in terms of back troubles. Basically, it is a problem of over-nutrition and under-activity — two contributory factors which we have discussed already at some length in the preceding chapters — and it needs little imagination to appreciate that any increase in body weight will impose unnecessary strain not only on the supporting tissues and discs of the spine but on the hips and knees also.

Nor do the harmful effects end there, for any increase in fatty tissue is almost invariably coincidental with a reduction in muscle bulk. As a result, the increased weight-burden has to be supported and transported by a weakened muscular system, with a consequentially greater susceptibility to injury and strain.

Moreover, since the abdomen is one of the main areas in which excess fatty tissue tends to be deposited, the resulting distension will exert a forward and downward pull on the lower spine, and so accentuate any existing distortion of the lumbar curve.

We cannot conclude our review of the predisposing causes of back troubles without a brief reference to the potentially harmful effects of prolonged mental stress. Whatever its causes — apprehension, anxiety, worry, fear, anger, emotional upsets, are but a few — the end result is to cause muscular tension and raised blood-pressure and to inhibit the complex processes of digestion and assimilation. These emotions are all components of the instinctive 'fight or flight' reactions which the body initiates in order to protect itself in a threatening situation, and once the danger is past normal functions would be resumed and physical and systemic equilibrium would be quickly restored. When, however, as is the case in many of the unnatural environmental, financial, and emotional situations with which many people now have to cope, the stressful conditions persist from day to day, week to week, and month to month, the resulting disruption of bodily functions can have far-reaching consequences in terms of bodily health.

Sustained muscular tension can cause circulatory constriction which will further increase the strain on the heart imposed by the raised blood-pressure. At the same time, the digestive functions will be seriously impaired because the secretion of gastric juices will be suspended. As a result, not only will the distribution of nutrients to the bodily tissues be impaired, but the passage of food residues through the alimentary canal will be slowed down, causing increasing abdominal distension and constipation. If this disruption is allowed to continue, congestion and inflammation of the delicate mucous membranes which line the intestines can lay the foundations for the more serious degenerative disorders such as peptic ulcerations, diverticulosis and haemorrhoids (piles).

In the context of our review of the causes of backache, any factor which contributes to abdominal distension will inevitably impose strain on the lumbar spine, and backache is a symptom which frequently presents itself in those who suffer from constipation and haemorrhoids, as it does, of course, in pregnancy and certain gynaecological disorders.

From what has been said in the preceding pages it will be appreciated that there are many factors which can weaken the tissues which support the spinal column and so make them susceptible to strain or injury, but it is almost invariably carelessness or sheer ignorance which are to blame for the sudden and dramatic breakdown which is responsible for so much agonizing pain and incapacity. It is to these 'trigger' factors that we shall now turn our attention.

6.

The final straws

I have stressed in a previous chapter that the human
body has a very considerable reserve of strength which
enables it to withstand a great deal of abuse and
misuse, but this characteristic can prove a mixed
blessing. By lulling us into a sense of false security, we
are encouraged to take liberties and impose ever-
increasing physical demands on our supporting tissues
until the day comes when, due perhaps to a combination of circumstances, the weakest link in the structural chain finally gives way. It is the old familiar story
of the final straw which breaks the camel's back, and
all too often the results can prove quite disastrous and
extremely painful.

Anyone who has attended an athletics meeting or
watched sprinters in action on television will probably
have seen a competitor in full flight suddenly veer off
the track and roll in agony on the ground clutching a
thigh or calf — the result of what is termed 'a pulled
muscle'. What has happened is that in exerting the
tremendous explosive effort needed to drive his body

forward the runner has imposed an intolerable strain on the contracting muscle, some of the fibres of which have ruptured — usually at the point where they are spliced into the tough, unyielding tendon which anchors them to a bone.

If an experienced athlete, trained to the highest degree of physical fitness, can suffer such an injury it is not surprising that lesser mortals should so frequently come to grief when imposing rather less severe demands on tissues which have not been conditioned to anything approaching the same degree as those of the athlete.

Especially vulnerable are those who participate in seasonal sports and other physical activities and who all too often allow enthusiasm to get the better of discretion when resuming active participation after a lapse of several months. Professional sportsmen, with all their specialized training facilities and the expert supervision of trainers and physiotherapists, regularly provide the sporting journalists with headline stories when they are unable to meet their commitments because of groin-strains, hamstring injuries, and various other disabilities. Such misfortunes are, therefore, even more likely to befall the amateur enthusiast.

The start of a new football, rugby, hockey, tennis, or cricket season invariably signals a surge of patients to the osteopaths' and physiotherapists' treatment couches as muscles, tendons, and joints are suddenly subjected to gross misuse and abuse with very little preparatory conditioning after the relatively undemanding activities of the off-season.

Shoulders, elbows, wrists, hips, knees, and ankles

are wrenched, strained and twisted, but it is the spine to which the limbs are attached which serves as the main support and fulcrum for all the complex physical contortions demanded by the various sporting activities. It is a tribute to the strength and durability of the human back-bone that it is able to withstand the repeated and heavy assaults that are imposed upon it, and usually it requires a combination of potentially harmful factors to bring about a breakdown.

It is common knowledge that most synthetic and natural materials are most easily broken or torn when they are subjected to low temperatures, and the muscles, tendons, and ligaments of the body are no exception to this rule. Failure to go through a programme of preliminary warming-up movements is probably one of the most frequent predisposing factors in sports injuries, and anyone who imposes a sudden burst of physical activity without proper graduated preparation is likely to suffer very painful consequences.

The risk is, of course, very much increased if, as is so often the case, participants in winter sports such as soccer, rugby, hockey, and cross-country running, change out of warm clothing into flimsy sporting kit which affords minimal warmth, leave the shelter of the clubroom and stand about in chilling rain, snow, or wind waiting for the starting whistle or gun before bursting into explosive activity. The imposition of violent muscular contraction on cold, inelastic tissues is an act of sheer madness and the surprising thing is that so many of the perpetrators do so with apparent impunity. Again, it is the very durability of the structural components of the human organism and its remarkable ability to withstand the demands imposed upon it that lulls us into a blissful sense of false security and encourages us to take increasing liberties with our bodies.

It is not only the young and athletic who are guilty in this respect, for the recurring epidemic of seasonal 'bad backs' suffered by gardeners and do-it-yourself enthusiasts bears eloquent witness to the fact that some people never learn the lessons of painful experience.

Easter is traditionally the time when men and women of all ages experience a sudden and irresistible urge to double-dig their vegetable plots and allotments, shift countless kilos of compost from the bins to various parts of the garden, launch a relentless assault on weeds, and dig up or transplant the burgeoning occupants of the flower-beds. Joints, muscles and tendons which have been cosseted by virtual hibernation throughout the winter months are suddenly subjected to hours of digging, lifting, carrying, bending and twisting, resulting, at best, in several days of painful joints and aching muscles, and, at worst, the sudden agonizing pain which signals a pulled muscle or crippling disc lesion.

The same seasonal rush of blood to the head impels householders of all ages and both sexes to spring-clean their homes and move furniture around as they clamber on chairs and steps stripping walls, washing down ceilings and then wielding paint and paste brushes for days on end, often rising with the dawn and working late into the night in response to the primeval urge to refurbish the 'nest' in preparation for the new mating season!

In the process, joints and soft tissues are subjected to

severe and unaccustomed strains, while the spine is bent, extended, and twisted to a degree that far exceeds anything that would be imposed on it in the course of normal daily activities.

A special hazard faces young married couples with the arrival of a new baby. Superimposed on the emotional stress which is generated by the event is the increasing physical strain entailed in lifting and carrying a growing and often demanding infant. Few women have the strength which would enable them to cope with the strains imposed on them during the nine months of pregnancy without at least an occasional bout of back pain, and all too often the resultant weakness is perpetuated by the additional demands imposed on them during the early years of the child's life.

During this period the father is not entirely immune from the risk of back injuries, although the danger-period in his case comes rather later in the child's formative years when swinging from the arms, tossing in the air, and similar activities are demanded of him. It is not so much the weight of the child — no more than 18kg (40lb) perhaps — that constitutes a potential hazard but the nature of the activity and the tremendous leverage forces which it imposes on the spine and its supporting tissues.

On a more prosaic level, there are a host of seemingly innocuous domestic and workaday activities which can lay a man or woman low with an acute attack of lumbago, sciatica, or some other variation on the backache theme. Among a long list of potential victims are:

- The factory or shop-worker who lifts a heavy object without due regard for anatomical and postural considerations.
- The passenger in a car whose neck and shoulder muscles are exposed to a cold draught and who is then jolted by sudden braking.
- The week-end golfer who, on the first tee, attempts the sort of drive that might daunt even a top professional.
- The housewife who attempts to turn a heavy and cumbersome mattress without assistance.
- The individual who fails to notice a kerb or step and lands heavily on one foot.
- The person who over-reaches when attempting to lift a heavy object off a high shelf.
- Finally, what is possibly the most trivial incident which can be responsible for some quite severe back lesions — the simple act of sneezing or coughing.

There is no doubt that every doctor, osteopath and physiotherapist could add even more bizarre case-histories to this list, but in almost every one of them some degree of ignorance or thoughtlessness and some lack of physical fitness will have been a major contributory factor in triggering off the ultimate breakdown.

7.

The doctor's dilemma

An extensive survey conducted by a responsible consumer organization has shown that of several thousand back-pain sufferers who were consulted, sixty per cent had sought help through the National Health Service, but nearly a quarter of these were dissatisfied with the treatment they received. This implies that more than half of all back-pain victims have reservations concerning their doctor's ability to help them and have been, or have become, disillusioned with regard to medical treatment.

The most frequently expressed reason for dissatisfaction was that doctors in general do not know enough about the nature and causes of back pain and how it should be treated, and there is little doubt that these misgivings are widely shared by the public at large.

In order to understand why such a regrettable situation should have come about it needs to be recognized that present-day medical practice is almost entirely drug-orientated. Consequently, when a patient consults a doctor, he or she has been conditioned to expect to be given a prescription which will be handed in at the local pharmacy in exchange for a bottle of medicine or a packet of pills or tablets.

The dilemma which faces the G.P. is that he is only too well aware that any form of medication which he can prescribe will afford only temporary *relief* from the painful symptoms but will do nothing to *cure* his patient. He knows, also, that unlike many common ailments, backache does not usually 'go away' in a week or two, which means that a demand for periodic repeat prescriptions is almost inevitable and that, sooner or later, the patient will become disenchanted with the 'treatment' he is receiving and demand something more effective.

'More effective' in this context can only mean a more potent analgesic — i.e. pain-relieving — drug, and as all medicines are known to give rise to harmful side-effects the prescription of something stronger will almost certainly mean something more potentially harmful to the patient. Moreover, the heavier the dosage and the longer the medication is continued, the greater will be the risks involved.

Aspirin is undoubtedly the best-known analgesic drug which is prescribed by doctors or purchased by the public from the chemists, supermarket, or general stores. Many millions of tablets are taken annually for the relief of a wide range of ailments including headache, toothache, fevers, neuralgia, muscle pains, and arthritis, and for many years it was regarded as a completely safe form of medication.

As the years went by, however, and public demand for the 'harmless household remedy' increased astronomically, disturbing reports began to appear in the medical press indicting aspirin as a cause of a variety of symptoms including dizziness, tinnitus (head-noises), profuse perspiration, nausea, vomiting, and mental confusion. One of the more serious toxic effects which is attributed to the drug, and which can occur with even small doses, is irritation and congestion of the delicate mucous membrane which lines the stomach, causing dyspepsia, ulceration, and erosion of the tissues and bleeding. It is believed that some blood-loss will occur in 10 per cent of patients who are treated with aspirin, regardless of the form in which it is taken, and that in time it may cause a type of anaemia.

Other analgesic drugs such as paracetamol and phenacatin which have been used as an alternative to, or in combination with, aspirin have also proved harmful to a greater or lesser degree.

Procaine injections have been used to relieve the more severe and disabling back pains, but although this is claimed to be one of the least toxic local anaesthetics it can cause a number of side-effects, and even death, in patients who are abnormally sensitive to the drug. Although the injection affords very rapid pain-relief, its effects are rather transitory.

As an alternative to injected and ingested drugs, sufferers from back pains and muscle strains are sometimes advised to use balms, sprays, creams, and liniments, the main effect of which is to generate heat in the affected areas and increase blood-circulation in the tissues. Some degree of temporary relief may be achieved by these methods, but the application of hot compresses, hot-water bottles, etc., has a similar effect and is more economical.

In really obstinate cases of back pain the patient may be advised to resort to wearing a supporting collar or corset, depending upon the site of the spinal disorder. Here again, some degree of relief from pain may be achieved by preventing movement of the affected vertebrae, but the enforced immobility can cause muscular atrophy, adhesions, and loss of tone in the supporting tendons with resulting weakness and increased susceptibility to subsequent strain when the support is eventually removed.

Surgery is the last desperate resort in cases of protracted back pain such as may be caused by a severe disc lesion, but whatever technique may be employed by the surgeon, and however skilfully he may perform the operation, there can be no guarantee of lasting benefit and there will almost certainly be some degree of permanent disability.

The inability of the family doctor to offer more positive advice and effective treatment when faced with a case of persistent back pain is probably no less frustrating to the G.P. than it is to his patient. The shortcomings of medical training are the limiting factor, inasmuch as the curriculum is heavily biased towards the conception that the doctor's primary function is to allay symptoms, with little or no regard for their causes. Consequently, when the G.P. is presented with a particular symptom or group of symptoms his first reaction is to append a name to the patient's condition so that he can then reach for his prescription pad and select from the thousands of drugs which are listed in his medical pharmacopoeia the one which appears to offer the best chance of relieving the troublesome symptom — aspirin for headache; and antacid for indigestion; a laxative for constipation; and antibiotic for bronchitis.

From the doctor's point of view it is a simple, convenient, conveyor-belt system which enables him to cope with a waiting-room full of patients in the limited time that he can allocate between his other commitments, and it may well be argued that without any such time-efficient procedure the National Health Service could not possibly continue to function.

The fallacy of such an argument lies in the fact that because drugs merely suppress symptoms and nothing is done to identify and remove their causes, a recurrence of the same problem or possibly a more serious complication is virtually inevitable, with a recurring demand upon the doctor's time. It is not surprising, therefore, that what was launched in 1946 as a National *Health* Service has deteriorated into a National *Disease* Service, the cost of which has rocketed year after year to its present astronomical level.

Public disillusionment with orthodox medicine is becoming increasingly prevalent, as is clearly exemplified by the fact that, in the review to which I referred earlier, more than 50 per cent of all patients interviewed had either been dissatisfied with the medical treatment they had received or had sought help outside the N.H.S.

The reason is not difficult to understand: the medical profession is no longer able to command the blind faith which was vested in it in the first half of the twentieth century and which, slowly but surely, has been whittled away by a growing public awareness of its limitations and failings. Increasingly, they are being asked questions to which they have no answer, or which they would prefer not to have to answer, such as 'How can this drug cure my complaint?' and 'Will it have any harmful side-effects?'

In this respect, back-pain sufferers have good reason for scepticism because so many of their number have been told by doctors and 'specialists' that they do not know the causes of the disability and that they may just have to go on taking the pills and learn to live with their problems.

More than two thousand years ago Hippocrates — the 'Father of Medicine' — was insisting that the doctor's primary consideration at all times should be to do no harm to his patient. Sadly, because modern medicine has allowed itself to become so heavily subjected to domination by the huge international drug cartels there is scarcely a doctor today who could claim total observance of that edict.

Dogged conservatism and a refusal to accept new ideas, even when they emanate from members of its own profession, is another characteristic of the medical establishment which has placed barriers in the way of progress. Only as a result of the growing pressure of public opinion has there been a grudging acceptance of the value of osteopathic manipulation in the treatment of structural lesions and the harmful potential of commercially denatured foods in regard to bodily health.

There is no more reason why a sufferer from backache should have to live with his disability than that a man who breaks a leg should have to spend the rest of his life on crutches.

Just as the human body has the innate capacity to

mend a broken bone or heal a wound, so it can repair a damaged disc or a torn ligament — so long as it is provided with the conditions and materials which it needs for the tasks in hand.

It is the latter subject to which we shall now turn our attention.

8.

Easing the pain

It is likely that most of those who are seeking help in these pages will have suffered from some form of back trouble for at least a few weeks and possibly for a very much longer period.

As a consequence, the very painful symptoms which are usually suffered during the acute stages immediately following a strain or injury will have eased to some extent and been replaced by the dull, nagging ache which characterizes the chronic stage.

Nevertheless, a recurrence of the acute symptoms is not uncommon, possibly as a result of some ill-advised activity which imposes further strain on the already weakened tissues. Should such an eventuality arise, or in order to ease the debilitating and more persistent aches and pains which plague the chronic sufferer, there are a number of techniques and precautions which will be helpful.

In the previous chapter I dealt at some length with the fallacies and dangers of relying on long-term medication, but I readily concede that the short-term use of analgesic drugs is justified in order to achieve rapid relief from the more severe and incapacitating back pains, particularly when they are causing loss of sleep. If a particular brand of drug has been obtained previously on prescription and has been found to be helpful it is probably wise to continue to use it, provided of course that the recommended dosage and frequency are not exceeded. Otherwise, aspirin or one of the proprietary analgesics may be tried, but *only* when, and for as long as, there is an urgent need.

At other times, or in order to reinforce the effect of medication, there is probably no more effective means of relieving pain than relaxing in a deep, hot bath for up to twenty minutes, provided, of course, that the nature and extent of the pain does not preclude such a procedure.

In the latter case, heat may be applied over the site of the pain by means of a hot compress — i.e. a pad or band of flannel or similar material, wrung out in hot water, placed in position and covered with a thick, dry towel in order to retain the heat as long as possible. An ordinary rubber hot-water bottle may be used in the same way, although care should be taken to avoid burning the skin, perhaps by interposing two or three layers of material under the bottle and removing them one by one as the water cools.

In cases where the pain is due to nerve compression or inflammation — e.g. sciatica and disc lesions — it may be found that more effective relief is obtained by applying a *cold* compress. Here, again, the pad or band of wet material is applied and covered with a thick, dry towel. The initial shock induced when the cold compress is applied will pass very quickly, and within a few minutes a soothing warmth will be generated. After an hour or so the compress may be renewed, or it may be removed and the area bathed with warm water and then dried.

If the cold compress is applied before retiring, the covering towel may be secured comfortably in place with safety-pins and kept on throughout the night. When it is removed in the morning it will have dried out completely, but the bathing routine should be carried out, and the compress material should be washed before it is re-used.

It is, of course, essential that all possible precautions should be taken to avoid exacerbation of the pain, and to this end careful thought needs to be given to the avoidance of postural strain. I pointed out in an earlier chapter the harmful potential of badly designed chairs, and need not stress, therefore, that the temptation to drop into a deep, low, soft-cushioned armchair or settee should be resisted — not only because of the resultant distortion of the spinal curves but also in order to avoid the excessive strain that is imposed on the muscles and ligaments when the time comes to haul oneself upright again.

Instead, a straight-backed, high chair should be chosen with comfortable but firm cushions on the seat and back-rest. Where lumbar pain is the problem, it will usually be found that flexing the hips by supporting the legs or feet on a stool or cushion will give added comfort. A chair with arm-rests, if one is available, will provide additional support with the further advantage that the hands and arms can be used to ease the strain on the legs and back when rising.

It is advisable to leave the chair from time to time —

say every half-hour or so — in order to ease the body upright and move around for a few minutes, otherwise there is a tendency for the joints to become 'set', making eventual movement more difficult and painful. Also, the resultant contraction and relaxation of the muscles will stimulate the circulation and prevent congestion caused by pooling of the blood in the lower limbs and abdomen.

Those who suffer from pain in the neck and upper spine, as well as some patients with lumbar pain, find that considerable relief is obtained by lying on the back on a carpeted floor, or on a folded blanket, with a low pillow or cushion supporting the base of the skull and another in the small of the back. The legs also may be supported with a cushion under the knees.

Indeed, this is a position which *all* sufferers should adopt for at least half an hour daily, and for even longer periods when circumstances permit — e.g. during the usually quiet hour or so following the evening meal once the domestic chores have been taken care of and the more insistent demands of younger members of the family have been met.

Otherwise, from the time we rise in the morning until we retire to bed at night — whether we be moving or stationary, standing, sitting or kneeling — many areas of the muscular system will be in the state of residual tension which is necessary to maintain balance and support the not inconsiderable weight of the head. As a consequence, the muscles of the neck, shoulder-girdle and spine may be kept in a state of unremitting contraction for hours on end throughout the day with the result that they become increasingly thickened and fibrous — a state of affairs which, with the passage of time, will almost inevitably lead first to muscular disorders such as fibrositis, stiffness, and reduced mobility, and later to the degenerative changes which lead to crippling arthritis and disc lesions.

As was explained in an earlier chapter, the supply of essential cell nutrients to all bodily tissues is very largely dependent upon an unhampered circulatory system which relies for its efficiency on the regular contraction and relaxation of the muscles which surround the blood-vessels. When, therefore, the muscles in any part of the body are maintained in a state of prolonged contraction the blood-supply to adjacent tissues is likely to be impaired to some extent, restricting the transmission of oxygen and other essential nutrients and allowing carbon-dioxide and waste products to accumulate.

In order to appreciate the extent of the unconscious muscular tension involved even when we are sitting comfortably in a chair reading this book it is only necessary to allow the hands to drop into the lap, the shoulders to relax completely, the wrists and fingers to go limp, and the head to fall forward onto the chest.

Even when this has been done it is likely that small areas of residual tension may still persist — the teeth may be clenched together, the abdominal muscles may be tensed, and the toes may be flexed. In order to achieve the optimum degree of relaxation, therefore, it is necessary to introduce into the daily routine a regular period in which one consciously, *and conscientiously*, releases the muscular tension that has built up in the performance of one's mental and physical activities. It is a simple procedure which will pay considerable dividends not only in terms of the relief of back pain and stiffness but also in the enhancement of systemic health and physical fitness.

The first essential — and probably the most difficult to achieve at first — is to eliminate as far as possible all sources of possible distraction and to provide an atmosphere that is conducive to physical and mental relaxation. The room should be comfortably warm and the curtains should be drawn to exclude extraneous noise. Certainly, the television should be switched off and lighting should be subdued, although soothing music is helpful provided that the equipment will not need attention during the time allocated for relaxation.

The position to be adopted is the same as that already specified — lying supine on a firm base with the minimum of support for the head and knees. The arms may rest at the sides or be lightly crossed on the chest. Breathing should be slow and rhythmic — not forced — and the eyes should be closed. The thoughts should be centred on the memory or imagination of a pleasant relaxed experience, such as lying alone in the sun on a warm, sandy beach with only the gentle lapping of the waves and occasional sea-bird calls breaking the silence; or stretched out on a new-mown lawn with the smell of flowers and the rustle of trees. Keep following this line of thought to ensure that there can be no intrusion of more mundane cares.

Once the mood of mental tranquility has been established, a process which should occupy no more than five minutes or so, the process of achieving physical relaxation can be commenced.

First squeeze the eyes, lips and jaws tightly shut, hold for a few seconds, then allow them to relax completely, keeping the eyes lightly closed but allowing the jaws to drop slightly and the lips to part slightly.

Next, the neck: raise the head off its support and press the tip of the nose forward and upward as far as possible, then relax the tensed muscles and allow the head to fall back to its former position.

Continue the same tense/relax procedures progressively with the shoulder-girdle, the arms and hands, the abdomen, the buttocks, thighs, calves, feet and the toes, concentrating on each group of muscles in turn but taking care to maintain relaxation in the areas which have been attended to previously.

Finally, having recognized the sensation of true muscular relaxation, tense quite strongly, but without undue strain, all the muscle groups simultaneously, and, *provided that it does not cause or increase any existing pain*, arch the back off the floor for a few seconds, then release *all* the tension and allow the head, limbs, and trunk to 'flop' back into full relaxation.

When the procedure has been completed and the maximum possible degree of relaxation has been achieved, return to the original state of peaceful contemplation and maintain it for the desired length of time.

It is unlikely that in the early stages full physical relaxation and mental detachment will be achieved and maintained, but each repetition should bring an increasing range of conscious control over muscles which, previously, had remained obstinately in a state of habitual tension. At the end of the relaxation session care should be taken to avoid imposing unnecessary strain on any group of muscles, especially those which support the back. It is always a good plan to limber up gradually after any period of inactivity in order to stimulate the blood-supply to the muscles and prepare them for renewed action.

To this end, a few minutes should be allowed during which the head is rotated gently on the neck, the shoulders are shrugged, the arms, hands, and fingers are moved in various directions, and the hips and knees are alternately flexed and extended — first one leg, then the other, and finally both together but taking care to keep the feet resting on the floor so as to avoid undue strain. Breathe deeply throughout the routine so that both the chest and the abdomen are made to distend and then subside.

When rising from the floor, you should first draw up your knees onto the abdomen — or as far as possible without causing pain or strain — before rolling over on to one side and then onto the knees so that the arms can be used to help support and lift the body into the upright position.

The latter procedure should be carefully adhered to even if the relaxation session is interrupted by an unexpected telephone call or ring at the doorbell.

Similar precautions should be observed when rising in the morning — loosening-up and then rolling to the edge of the bed and swinging the legs over the side, resting for a few seconds in the sitting position before easing the body erect.

Some types of back pain are more severe after a night's rest and those who suffer in this way should consider whether a sagging or too-soft mattress or spring-base may be causing lateral distortion of the spine. Replacing these items can of course prove to be a costly experiment, and a cheaper and often quite effective alternative is simply to place a sheet of ply-wood or hardboard between the mattress and the base. Where space and domestic circumstances permit the same effect can be achieved even more cheaply by placing the mattress on the floor.

For the majority of back sufferers, the most comfortable sleeping position is on one side with one or both knees drawn up. It is important, however, that the pillow should be just high enough to support the head without causing a kink in the neck or upper spine.

If the most comfortable position is side-lying with the lower leg straight and the other flexed, it may be helpful to place a small pillow in the bed to take the weight of the uppermost leg and foot and also to prevent the pelvis from rotating and imposing strain on the lumbar spine.

Those who prefer to sleep lying face-upwards can also reduce strain on the lower back by placing a pillow under the knees, thus flexing the hips slightly.

The value of massage in the relief of back pain is very widely recognized, but unfortunately there are very few sufferers who can avail themselves of the services of a skilled operator. Facilities within the National Health Service are extremely limited, and those who are fortunate enough to be offered a weekly appointment with a physiotherapist are likely to find that the benefits obtained are largely aborted by the effort and strain involved in travelling to and from the local hospital and possibly having to wait for some time before being called for treatment.

Nevertheless, when the initial acutely painful symptoms have subsided sufficiently, and where it is possible to enlist the services of a relative or friend who is armed with a little practical knowledge and a reasonable degree of physical fitness, a great deal can be achieved in soothing pain and hastening recovery. The following simple procedures do, however, impose a degree of strain on the operator and should not be attempted, therefore, by the elderly or anyone, male or female, who has a history of any kind of back trouble or a rheumatic condition.

All that is needed is a reasonably firm bed or divan on which the patient can lie at full length, a large bath-towel or an old sheet to cover and protect the bedclothes, and a little vegetable oil. Any kind will do, although olive oil is frequently used. One of the special massage oils or embrocations may be substituted if preferred, but care needs to be taken in some cases because the stronger brands can cause inflammation and soreness of the skin in certain sensitive individuals if used too freely. Apart from generating a comforting warmth, the distinctive aroma which they emit has a psychologically therapeutic value in those patients who, from childhood perhaps, have been brought up to believe in the healing properties of 'something out of a bottle'!

A small supply of large tissues or a few sheets from a kitchen roll should be available to clean any residual oil from the hands and skin at the conclusion of the treatment.

The treatment consists of four separate phases, and because of the abnormal physical demands which are imposed on the operator's muscular system it is suggested that, initially, a total of only 20 minutes should be allocated — i.e. 5 minutes for each stage — with a progressive extension up to 40 minutes — 10 minutes per stage — if time and physical resources permit. The room should be comfortably warm, and the oil and the operator's hands should also be warmed.

Phase 1.
With the patient lying face-downward close to the edge of the bed, and head resting comfortably close to the foot of the bed, the operator stands at the foot of the bed and lightly oils the patient's back.

Then, bending forwards and exerting firm but not heavy pressure, the hands stroke alternately and slowly down the length of the patient's spine from the neck to the coccyx, the object being to stimulate the circulation and relax the patient.

Phase 2.
From the same positions, and with the patient encouraged to 'let go' and release all tension from the spinal muscles, the operator places a thumb on either side of the central bony prominence of the spine at the base of the skull and, pressing firmly, moves the thumbs slowly apart for approximately three inches *across* the fleshy muscle fibres. The thumbs are then moved two inches or so further down the spine and the movement is repeated, moving successively downward until the full length fo the spine has been treated.

Phase 3.
From the same starting positions, and working from the neck, the well-oiled thumbs are slid simultaneously down the length of the spine pressing firmly into the bulky spinal muscles. Return to starting position and repeat.

Phase 4.
Repeat phase 1, then dry the hands and skin with the tissues.

Although the primary purpose of these soft-tissue techniques is to relieve pain and congestion, they also play a very valuable role in releasing tension in the powerful back muscles, particularly where they have gone into spasm as a result of strain or injury.

A regular daily treatment will therefore pay very substantial dividends when circumstances permit, but even a once- or twice-weekly session is well worth the time and effort involved.

9.

Repair and reconstruction

Only a small proportion of 'bad backs' is due to disease
in the accepted sense of the term — e.g. kidney disease,
spinal caries, tumours, and gynaecological disorders
— and in these cases the associated organic and
systemic symptoms will almost certainly have necessi-
tated professional investigation and produced a clear-
cut diagnosis.

The vast majority of back pains are the result of
strain and injury and so in considering a therapeutic
approach we must think in terms of repair and reconstruction rather than of 'cure'. There are no germs
or viruses to be killed by antibiotics, no coughs or
sneezes to be suppressed with decongestants, and no
stomach pains to be eased with antacids, which is one
of the main reasons why the patient who seeks medical
advice is so frequently given a prescription for aspirins
or one of the other analgesics and simply told to go
home, rest, and keep warm.

In its limited way, of course, that is sound advice,
but it ignores the vitally important 'sow's ear' factor —

that the body needs the right materials in the right combinations and quantities if it is to rebuild damaged tissues with the maximum speed and efficiency.

As I have stressed in an earlier chapter, the spine and its associated tissues are but a part of an organism of almost unimaginable complexity which can only function properly as a *single entity* of which each component, no matter how large or small, is interdependent upon all the others.

The saying that a chain is only as strong as its weakest link sums up the situation to perfection so far as the human body is concerned. Each individual cell — which is the ultimate component of every organ — is linked directly or indirectly to the other cells by the nerves, the blood, and the connective tissues, and only when there is complete harmony throughout the organism can anyone claim to be truly healthy.

Sadly, such a state of perfection is virtually impossible to achieve in the 'civilized' world which we have created for ourselves, but that is certainly not a valid reason why any of us should accept the not uncommon edict that nothing can be done to remedy so many of the ills which beset us and that we must 'keep taking the pills and learn to live with it'!

Backache, as I have already insisted, is due in the vast majority of cases to a fundamental defect in the structural integrity of the tissues, and just as the fabric of a building will erode and crumble if poor-quality bricks and mortar are used in its construction, so the tendons and ligaments which form a major structural component of the spine will weaken and eventually break down if the cells of which they are formed are sub-standard.

Throughout life, these cells are subject to a never-ending process of breakdown and renewal, and the only materials which the body can utilize for the purposes of growth and repair are those which it receives via the food we eat, the liquids we drink, and the air we breathe.

It is to these three sources that we must therefore turn our attention when we come to identify the causes of systemic and organic breakdown and to determine what are the logical steps that must be taken if we are to make good the damage and prevent a recurrence.

Unfortunately, the word 'diet' has come to have rather unattractive connotations in the minds of many people who think of it nowadays only in terms of restriction and deprivation — even starvation — whereas the Greek word from which it derives meant 'a way of life'. It is imperative, therefore, that it is clearly understood that since, for the sake of simplicity and clarity, we must make frequent use of the word in this chapter, we do so in the wider, constructive sense.

Certainly, there is no possible justification for assuming that a well-balanced diet of healthful, wholefoods must of necessity be less satisfying or attractive than the conglomeration of processed and chemicalized products — they do not deserve to be termed 'foods' — which it is now widely accepted are largely responsible for the ever-increasing burden of ill health and affliction which bedevils 'civilized' industrialized communities.

Indeed, once the simple, basic rules of nutrition are understood it will be found that the transition from 'orthodox' feeding to a wholefood regimen need entail relatively few changes in the domestic catering arrangements. It is accepted, however, that long-established prejudices and preferences will need to be abandoned, but with the exercise of a little patience and self-discipline even the most deeply ingrained habit patterns can be changed in a relatively short period of time.

The most fundamental change involves the staple foods — the cereals and proteins. These are the items which account for by far the greatest proportion of the average household's weekly food budget, and which, over the years, have been subjected to massive exploitation by the multi-national food-processing companies.

White flour forms the basis or a major constituent of a vast range of tinned and packeted foods which are then flavoured, preserved, coloured, and manipulated in many other ways with the aid of white sugar, salt, and an extraordinary conglomeration of chemical agents which are identified by meaningless code numbers or unpronounceable multi-syllabic laboratory names.

A study of the labels on many of the widely advertised products which constitute a considerable bulk of the supermarket stock-in-trade will reveal the extent to which commercial expediency and profit motivation have virtually extinguished considerations of nutritional values. Appeal to the eye and palate is achieved with the aid of colourful packaging and exotic names, but in many cases what little food value they may have when they eventually reach the dining table is derived not from the contents of the tin or packet but from the milk or other additional ingredients with which they are prepared or served by the housewife.

The extent to which the products of the laboratory are being used to replace, imitate, or enhance the flavour, colour, texture, and various other characteristics of basic foods is revealed by a research project carried out by the British Consumers' Association which revealed that out of every ten packaged food products which were examined in a supermarket no less than eight contained chemical additives of one kind or another. For the purposes of their survey they visited 10 branches of several well-known chain stores from each of which they purchased 17 of the more popular packaged food items, and it was found that the labels listed between 31 and 106 additives.

Some of the products — e.g. salmon and shrimp paste, canned garden peas and black cherry yogurt — had relatively low scores of 3 additives or less, but at the other end of the scale they found that certain items such as orangeades, tomato soup, beef sausages, ice-cream, margarine, and sweet pickles scored up to 9 additives, while one sample of chocolate Swiss roll was found to contain 13, and a Black Forest gateau had a staggering 20! Indeed, even these numbers could have been higher because some of the lists on the labels contained a single term, such as 'flavourings' which could well have implied the use of more than one substance.

For example, the gateau contained 3 emulsifiers (E475, E471 and E322), 3 preservatives (E211, E202 and E220), 2 stabilizers (E412 and E407), no less than 6 colours (E102, E124, E122, E142, E151 and chocolate brown HT), as well as modified starch, citric acid, and unspecified flavourings, some of which were used more than once in the sponge, filling or decoration.

Bearing in mind that human metabolic function is dependent on the maintenance of a very delicately controlled balance between the *naturally occurring* chemical and mineral components of whole foods, it is not difficult to appreciate the disruption that must be caused when such an extraordinary mixture of *foreign* chemicals is ingested day after day. And as if this gastronomic abuse were not enough of a health hazard, it has to be remembered that much of the remaining bulk of the daily food intake has been refined, processed, and cooked to such an extent that many of the vitamins, minerals, and other essential nutrients which were present in the original product have been either removed or destroyed.

Again, I have digressed from the subject of repair and reconstruction in order to impress upon the reader the fundamental principle of natural healing — namely, that strong, healthy tissues can only be constructed if we provide the body with carefully selected, high-quality materials in the right quantities and combinations. It is not enough merely to be told what needs to be done in order to solve the problems of backache. Of equal or perhaps even greater importance is a clear understanding of *why* the various measures are necessary and how they complement each other in relieving distressing symptoms, rebuilding damaged tissues and then strengthening and reinforcing the vulnerable areas as a safeguard against a recurrence of the problems at a later date.

The knowledge that something can be done, and is being done, to restore pain-free mobility and the capacity to enjoy a normal, active life provides the necessary incentive to change old, harmful habits of feeding and living — to make whatever short-term sacrifices may be required in order to achieve and maintain long-term objectives. In this context, the use of the word 'sacrifices' is perhaps inappropriate because the changes which need to be made mean no more than the adoption of constructive, beneficial habits in place of destructive and harmful practices.

When any repair job is being undertaken, it is advisable to 'tidy up the site' and clear away any accumulation of rubbish and unwanted materials, and this preliminary is no less important when we are preparing to deal with damaged or defective bodily tissues.

We have explained already that faulty nutrition and physical inactivity cause circulatory congestion and so impair the removal of toxic residues from the tissues, and our first priority, therefore, is to initiate a crash course of cleansing procedures — a thorough three-week physiological spring-clean which will enable the body's eliminative organs to carry out their respective functions as speedily and efficiently as possible.

For this purpose, as will be explained more fully in Appendix A on page 111, the diet is restricted for the first seven days to what naturopaths regard as the cleansing and detoxifying foods — the fruits, vegetables, and salads which are a rich source of vitamins and other essential nutrients and which contain a high proportion of pure, cleansing liquid and sufficient fibre to motivate the digestive system and stimulate elimination via the bowels.

During the second and third weeks the diet is progressively amplified by gradually increasing the quantities of fruit and salads and including a main meal of steamed vegetables to which a protein dish is eventually added.

At the same time, a carefully moderated programme of deep-breathing and remedial exercises is introduced with the double objective of stimulating the circulation, toning up the muscles, mobilizing the spinal joints and breaking down any existing adhesions.

For those who are overweight, this part of the treatment programme will allow the body to break down and burn up the surplus fatty tissues and thus gradually reduce the excessive load which the body's supporting structures have had to bear.

Having completed the initial tissue-cleansing process, our next concern is to provide the body with the materials that it needs in order to restore physical strength and enable its vital organs to function efficiently.

Clearly, because individual nutritional needs vary very considerably from one person to another and even in the same person from day to day, it is not possible to prescribe a dietary plan which will be universally acceptable. Apart from the very different requirements of men and women, there are many other variable factors which need to be considered, including age, physical activities, occupation, general health, and even changing weather conditions. Nevertheless, there is a simple formula which many naturopaths endorse and which allows individual quantitative adaptations while ensuring that the overall nutritional balance is maintained. It consists of planning the day's meals so that the main components are taken in an approximate ratio of 20 per cent carbohydrates (wholegrain cereals such as bread, rice, pasta, etc.), 20 per cent protein (meat, fish, cheese, nuts, eggs, etc.), and 60 per cent of the vitamin-rich, 'cleansing' fruits, vegetables and salads.

The specimen menus in Appendix B on page 117 will serve to illustrate how this principle is translated into practice, but although, as we have explained, the quantities of the various types of food can be adjusted within the formula to meet individual needs, it should be stressed that over-eating or indulgence in excessively bulky meals, even though they may consist of whole foods of the highest nutritional quality, will prove counter-productive in that the stomach and intestines will be overloaded and the digestive and assimilative functions will be impaired.

Most people today tend to 'eat by the clock' and as a result we no longer experience true hunger which is Nature's signal that food is needed. Instead, we have developed a 'false appetite' which manifests itself as a *feeling* of hunger at set times throughout the day, and which all too often is appeased regardless of physiological needs. It is this ritual and socially motivated pattern of eating and drinking which is largely responsible for the increasing incidence of obesity and many of the other health problems with which this is associated.

The validity of this assertion can be put to the test quite easily by missing a meal occasionally, or simply having a snack of fresh fruit and perhaps a glass of water or dilute fruit juice. It is likely that once the hands of the clock have moved past the customary meal-time the false-appetite signal will have been switched off and there will be no further demand for food until the routine time comes for the next meal.

It is accepted that because of domestic and occupational commitments few of us are able to eat only when true hunger manifests itself, but by exercising self-discipline and having relatively small meals of simple whole foods, which are eaten slowly and masticated thoroughly, the body will thrive and function far more efficiently and without any lack of energy or vital capacity.

I cannot stress too strongly the fact that habitually over-eating is counter-productive in terms of bodily health in so far as the digestive and assimilative systems are over-taxed and therefore unable to utilize essential nutrients. Consequently, a sensation of false hunger is generated, with the result that more food is consumed and gradually a vicious circle is created:

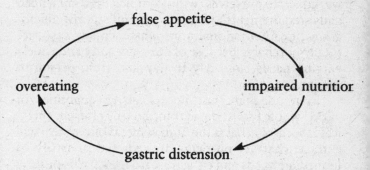

It is a state of affairs which explains why obviously over-fed and overweight individuals are often heard to complain that they are 'always hungry'. They are simply over-fed but undernourished — a situation which inevitably bodes ill in terms of their future health.

There is more than a grain of truth in the claim that, in the case of many people today, one half of what is eaten makes them healthy, while the other half makes their doctors wealthy! Nor is there a greater fallacy than the assertion that 'you cannot have too much of a good thing'!

By eating sparingly of simple, whole foods, and keeping more or less within the 20:20:60 formula, we shall ensure that our bodies are provided with an adequate and balanced diet containing a wide range of vitamins, minerals, proteins, carbohydrates, fats, fibre, and all the other essential nutrients in an easily digestible and assimilable form and in their correct proportions and combinations. It is not necessary to count calories or weigh individual portions, nor need we concern ourselves with complex 'recommended daily requirements' in terms of milligrams, micrograms, or international units which, in any case, are totally unreliable because of our constantly and widely varying needs from day to day and from person to person.

Given adequate but not excessive quantities of varied whole foods, the extraordinarily efficient chemical laboratory that is the human metabolic system will extract whatever nutrients are required to satsify its immediate needs and either discard the surplus or store it away for future use.

Simplicity and moderation, then, are the over-riding principles which should guide us in our choice of foods, and the specimen menus set out in Appendix B will provide a pattern which the reader can use and develop to meet his or her personal needs. Basically, the aim is to provide a good proportion of conservatively cooked or raw vegetables, fruits, and salads, together with only a moderate amount of wholegrain cereal foods and an equally moderate but *varied* protein element.

There is today, particularly among younger people, an increasing leaning towards vegetarianism which is generated in many cases by humanitarian considerations and a laudable desire to reduce the apalling level of animal exploitation which is implicit in the widespread adoption of battery and 'factory-farming' methods.

Naturopaths have always maintained that the human digestive system is designed primarily to deal with non-flesh foods. A comparison with the cats and other carnivores shows clearly that their teeth are well adapted to the functions of killing their prey and tearing its flesh, while the very short intestine ensures the speedy elimination of highly fermentable residues. Our own teeth are more suited to the functions of cutting and crushing seeds, roots, and fruits, before the residues pass more slowly along the very much more lengthy intestine.

It needs to be stressed, however, that those who have been accustomed all their lives to having an 'orthodox' diet, based on cooked foods and animal proteins, need to proceed with caution if they should be tempted to adopt a vegetarian regime. The sudden imposition of bulky, raw foods on the digestive system can cause a number of problems, especially if, as is frequently the case, meat dishes are abandoned in favour of more bulky proteins derived from a variety of beans and exotic seeds, and supplemented with cereal derivatives.

Such drastic changes need to be undertaken with circumspection as well as a reasonably clear appreciation of the nutritional characteristics of the substitute foods. A wise precaution, therefore, would be to obtain a good vegetarian cookery book offering a varied selection of recipes and menus. The catalogue issued by the publishers of this book contains a number of such works, a selection of which will be found on the shelves of most health food stores.

A study of these books will, I think, demonstrate that the adoption of a health-promoting, wholefood regimen can be accomplished without making costly and complex changes in the domestic catering arrangements. Indeed, the main difference between old shopping practices and the new is likely to be a reduction in the amount of costly processed, packeted, and tinned 'convenience' foods and a corresponding increase in the amount of fresh produce from the greengrocer. Such a change would, in fact, mean a welcome reduction in the catering budget for those who are fortunate enough to have garden space which can be utilized for the production of fresh vegetables and salads and perhaps even some varieties of fruits.

It will be found that for most families the main meal of the day will remain basically unchanged — e.g. a protein dish with two or three green or root vegetables or an occasional salad. Stodgy puddings and the 'ready-mixed' desserts should be avoided — preferably in favour of fresh or dried fruit, either raw or cooked. Fried or fatty foods should also be excluded.

It needs to be remembered that the vitamins and

minerals of which whole foods are such a valuable source are easily destroyed by excessive heat or by leaching when foods are boiled in a large quantity of water which is then poured down the sink. Such losses can, however, be minimized if conservative cooking methods are employed — namely steaming or braising or using a minimum quantity of water which is then used to make a soup or gravy.

Pressure-cooking may save time and fuel costs — though not as much as some makers claim — and this method is acceptable provided that the recommended cooking times are scrupulously observed. Because of the very high temperatures involved, even a relatively small error in timing can cause a disproportionately high destruction of some of the heat-sensitive vitamins, especially vitamin C. The same precautions should be observed when a microwave oven is used.

When it is necessary to cook food in general, but fruits and vegetables in particular, the guiding principle should be minimum time, minimum heat, and the minimum of water. It is advisable, also, to use stainless steel or enamelled pans for cooking purposes rather than those made from aluminium, because it is suspected that the latter metal may be leached into the food and be detrimental to health.

To the reader who has had little or no previous experience of the subject of nutrition and the vital part that it plays in the restoration and maintenance of bodily health and physical fitness, what has been proposed in these pages may well seem revolutionary and complicated. We suggest, therefore, that any such difficulties will be more readily resolved if the preceding chapters are re-read so that the main principles are more fully digested and assimilated.

Once this is achieved, a solid foundation will have been established on which weakened and damaged tissues can be rebuilt. Our next consideration is to explain what needs to be done to restore full mobility and ensure that the supporting structures of the spine are strengthened sufficiently to cope with any of the stresses and strains that may be imposed on them in future.

10.

Restoring strength and mobility

An inevitable consequence of any kind of backache is the sufferer's natural tendency to avoid the activities and types of movement which either cause or aggravate the pain, and because injured tendons and ligaments are invariably slow to heal there is often a protracted period during which the spine is maintained in a state of comparative immobility.

During this time, which rarely lasts for less than three or four weeks and may extend to several months, the disused muscles tend to atrophy and the ligaments lose their elasticity and become increasingly thickened and fibrous. Therefore, unless a conscious effort is made to rebuild the wasted muscles and break down the fibrous adhesions the patient's spine will become progressively more inflexible and susceptible to the degenerative changes which herald the onset of arthritis and other diseases which are such a common feature of the ageing process.

It is imperative, therefore, that once the more painful symptoms of backache have begun to ease a

programme of remedial exercises should be commenced and continued patiently and conscientiously
until all traces of weakness and stiffness have been
eliminated. Discretion will need to be observed initially to ensure that the weakened tissues are *coaxed*
back into action by relatively gentle, exploratory
movements — twisting, turning, and bending over a
limited but progressively extended range, ensuring
that the limit is set at any point where pain or strain
begins to manifest itself.

A characteristic of many types of backache is that,
regardless of duration — whether weeks or months —
the pain can vanish just as quickly as it started. When
this occurs, considerable restraint needs to be exer-
cised in order to guard against an over-impetuous
resumption of normal activities which is an un-
derstandable but very unwise reaction. In all cases of
convalescence — whether following an injury or any
kind of illness — there is no doubt that the simple
exercise of walking is by far the best and most natural
means of stimulating all the bodily systems and functions which will have been weakened by enforced rest.

As we have explained earlier in this book, a persistent lack of physical exercise has far-reaching effects
on the lungs, the circulation, the heart and the whole
metabolic system, and the best tonic we can take is a
regular, daily brisk walk combined with deep breathing.

With the feet parallel, the legs and arms swinging
rhythmically, the lungs expanding and contracting and
the diaphragm rising and falling, the 'muscle-pump'
will be set in motion forcing fresh, oxygenated blood
through the arteries to even the most remote parts of
the body, clearing away tissue debris and transporting

it to the cleansing and eliminating organs.

Depending upon physical capacity — or incapacity — it may be necessary to confine one's activities to no more than a gentle stroll of ten or fifteen minutes in the early stages, but the aim should be gradually to increase both pace and distance until, ideally, it is possible to achieve something in the region of a three-mile stint within an hour. Again, however, it is stressed that discretion *must* be observed and allowances made for such potentially limiting factors as age, weight, general health, and physical condition.

Those who have suffered a back-strain or injury should on no account be tempted into running or jogging for at least three months or even six, because these activities impose a rapidly recurring and quite considerable compression force on the joints and discs. For the same reason, it is advisable to wear well-fitting canvas shoes with a thick cushion sole if the exercise is taken on stone paving or any other very hard surface.

When walking — as indeed in all other activities — a comfortable, balanced posture should be maintained. It should be remembered that the act of walking consists simply of allowing the body to 'fall forward' and then moving the feet alternately in order to maintain equilibrium. The rigidly erect military marching posture adopted by soldiers on parade is anatomically incorrect and is conducive to muscular tension and strain.

Swimming is an excellent alternative to walking when the necessary facilities are available, provided that no attempt is made to force the pace. A slow, rhythmic action should be maintained and the session should be terminated immediately if any sign of pain or strain is experienced. Once out of the water, the body should be dried immediately and briskly, and the wet costume should be exchanged for warm clothing.

An exception to this rule may be made in hot, sunny weather when, after drying, it is permissible and beneficial to relax and sun-bathe, taking care, of course, to avoid over-exposure.

To complement the beneficial effects of the outdoor activities, some time should be set aside for a programme of remedial exercises designed to gradually stretch the contracted and thickened ligaments and break down any adhesions which may have formed.

The specific type of exercise and the duration of the session will of course need to be determined by the nature and extent of the spinal trouble but, again, the same precautions must be observed in regard to age, general condition, etc.

In Appendix C, on page 120, I have set out comprehensive programmes of exercises designed to mobilize either the lower trunk or the neck and upper spine, and they are arranged so as to be undertaken progressively. It is suggested that, as soon as the more painful symptoms have subsided, the appropriate early movements should be introduced cautiously. Begin gently and tentatively, and keep the range of movement well within comfortable limits, then increase it gradually and introduce the more demanding exercises as mobility is restored.

Back pain is without doubt the problem above all others in the resolution of which the services of an experienced osteopath are invaluable in order to achieve the speediest possible recovery. A skilled practitioner will be able to establish a reliable diagnosis of the nature and extent of the lesion and, after studying the patient's history, he will identify likely causes and give detailed personal advice regarding remedial exercises and other treatment measures which need to be adopted. In addition, he will of course use his manipulative skills and soft-tissue techniques in order to correct lesions and break down adhesions.

Unfortunately, these services are not at present available through the National Health Service, but practitioners can be located by referring to the local Yellow Pages telephone directory. Fees vary to some extent according to the location of the practice, but any doubts on this subject can be resolved by a telephone enquiry prior to making an appointment.

It is necessary to point out, however, that there is no officially recognized national register of qualified osteopaths and it is, in fact, possible for anyone to set up in practice regardless of the nature and length of training that has been undergone. The increasing public demand for osteopathic treament has led to a proliferation of 'schools' and 'colleges' offering courses of training of widely varying duration and ranging from a few months' postal tuition to four years or more of full-time study and clinical training. Two of the oldest establishments in the latter category are the British College of Naturopathy and Osteopathy, Frazer House, 6 Netherhall Gardens, London, NW3 5RR, and the British School of Osteopathy, 1–4 Suffolk Street, London, SW1 4HG. Graduates may be identified respectively by the letters MBNOA (Member of the British Naturopathic and Osteopathic Association) and MRO (Member of the Register of Osteopaths) after their names in the directory.

The services of a qualified osteopath are especially valuable in cases where a disc lesion is suspected.

11.

Now close the stable door!

It is surprising how many of the old saws or maxims are found to be especially relevant to the subject of the human spine and the pains and disabilities to which its misuse and abuse can give rise.

For example, 'familiarity breeds contempt' epitomizes the all-too-common failing of assuming that we can continue with impunity to impose on ourselves increasing stresses and burdens simply because we have never had an ache or pain in our lives.

By the same token, we are likely to remain blissfully unaware of the abnormal and accentuated curves which all too often are precursors of impending back troubles simply because that part of our anatomy is 'Out of sight, out of mind'!

Having therefore suffered and hopefully recovered from the invariably painful consequences of such thoughtlessness and neglect, it behoves us to paraphrase another of the old saws and close the stable door *before* the horse can bolt for a second time.

I have dwelt at some length in an earlier chapter

on the vital role which proper nutrition fulfils in building and maintaining strong and healthy tissues. I do not propose to labour the point further at this stage except to re-emphasize the over-riding necessity to avoid the dietetic shortcomings which are so largely responsible not only for the substandard ligaments, tendons, and muscular tissues which predispose to back troubles but also for many of the other organic and systemic afflictions which cause so much human misery and claim so many lives.

It is not necessary to become a food crank or fanatic in order to be well-nourished and healthy. All that is required is that a few old habits are modified and that the overall emphasis be shifted from processed and denatured 'convenience foods' to the basic, staple foods in their natural state — i.e. fresh vegetables, fruits, and salads, wholewheat bread and wholegrain cereals, and a varied choice of protein foods.

If one's normal feeding habits are based on the fundamental principles of simplicity and moderation, in conjunction with the 20:20:60 formula explained in Chapter 9, then there is no need for anyone to be deprived of the occasional pleasures of 'eating out' or of serving an 'orthodox' meal when playing host to friends. Exotic dishes can, however, be prepared just as easily from wholefood ingredients, with the aid of a little imagination and a good cookery book.

Second only to sound nutrition is the need to ensure that our bodies are used efficiently and economically in the performance of our varying daily activities. Those whose domestic and occupational commitments are of a mainly sedentary nature should remember that even when we are sitting down the lower vertebrae and discs are subjected to very considerable pressure, and the strain on the tendons and ligaments which support the trunk will be greatly increased if the spinal curves are accentuated by slumping forward or lounging backward. It is important, therefore, to ensure as far as possible that the desk or work-table is sufficiently high to allow the elbows to rest comfortably on the surface, and that the chair or bench has a padded seat that is deep enough to support the length of the thighs. Ideally, the back-rest should be angled correctly to fit into the small of the back and provide support just beneath the shoulder-blades, but failing this it may be possible to suspend a small, firm cushion so as to achieve the desired result.

Similar principles need to be observed by those who spend long periods at the wheel of a car or other vehicle. They should ensure not only that the back-rest is adjusted to the correct angle, but also that the pedals can be reached and operated without unnecessary strain. On long journeys, considerable tension can build up in the upper spine and shoulder-girdle which, besides causing stiffness and strain, can also inhibit the blood-supply to the brain. As a consequence, concentration can be impaired, followed by increasing drowsiness, and it is possible that such a train of events is responsible for some of the otherwise inexplicable accidents that befall motorists, lorry-drivers, etc. whose work entails long periods of motorway driving.

The best safeguard, of course, is to break the journey every two hours or so and loosen up the legs, arms, shoulders, and neck for five or ten minutes before resuming. If this is impracticable for any reason, some of the tension can be released by shrugging the shoulders vigorously for a few seconds, then stretching the neck and circling the head in both directions and turning it fully from side to side.

Shop workers, housewives, and others who are on their feet for much of the day should wear roomy, low-heeled shoes or even, when circumstances permit, discard shoes and stockings and walk in bare feet.

Every opportunity should be taken to keep moving, even if this means no more than shifting the weight of the body from one foot to the other in order to bring the 'muscle-pump' into operation and keep the blood from pooling in the legs and feet. Here, also, a conscious effort should be made to maintain the correct curvatures of the spine, and to prevent the shoulders and abdomen from sagging and the head from poking forward. The most comfortable standing position is with the hips and shoulders square, the feet about twelve inches apart and slightly splayed.

If a shopping-bag, brief-case, or other heavy object has to be carried for any length of time it should be transferred from one side to the other periodically, and the strain will be reduced if the handles can be looped over the shoulder or elbow.

Special care needs to be taken when lifting a heavy or bulky article from the floor. Very serious strain can be imposed on the spine if the trunk is bent forward from the waist with the knees almost straight. Instead, a squatting position should be adopted with the knees and hips flexed so that the spine may be kept reasonably straight. From this position, it is the powerful muscles of the thighs and buttocks which take most of the strain, while the leverage forces on the lower spine are reduced to a minimum.

Special precautions need to be taken also during the winter months to avoid overloading cold muscles and tendons, and clothing should be chosen carefully to ensure that vulnerable areas are adequately protected. A short jacket or other top garment which rides up when the wearer bends forward and leaves a gap above the waist-band of trousers or skirt can expose the lumbar spine to a chilling wind — one of the classic preconditions of backache to which gardeners and other outdoor workers so often succumb.

Some thought needs to be given also to the materials of which underclothes are made. Nylon and other synthetic fabrics are non-absorbent and have poor ventilation properties, which means that perspiration is trapped on the surface of the body instead of being allowed to evaporate and disperse. As a result the clothing becomes increasingly damp and clammy, and the wearer is therefore very susceptible to rapid chilling during any pause in physical activities, whether they be gardening, walking, or even more energetic pursuits. To minimize this type of health hazard, it is best to choose clothing made from cotton, wool, or some other natural fabric.

To enable the body's very efficient temperature-control mechanisms to function effectively care should be taken to ensure that all parts of the body are equally clothed and protected, particular when exposure to very cold winds is likely. During the warm months the aim should be to wear only the minimum amount of clothing necessary for comfort, choosing light and loose-fitting garments which allow the skin to breathe and perspiration to evaporate as quickly as possible.

Frequent indulgence in hot baths is a temptation

which should be resisted because of their weakening effect on the skin and the circulatory congestion which they induce. Civilized man is the only living creature which has acquired this habit — indeed, even the domesticated dog will show an instinctive reluctance to submit to even a moderately warm immersion, and yet will often plunge happily into cold water even in mid-winter.

Man, of course, has long since lost the covering of hair which protects other animals from the elements, but the healthy skin still secretes a protective substance which serves to keep the tissues supple and water-proof, filter out harmful radiation and repel harmful bacteria. Repeated washing or bathing in hot water and the use of chemical bath lotions, shampoos, and other detergent substances can have harmful effects which far outweigh any sensory or psychological benefits.

As has been explained in an earlier chapter, the health of the human body as a whole is dependent on the well-being of each and every tissue and organ. It behoves us, therefore, to avoid any practice which is in any way detrimental to any bodily part or function, and no matter how remote the connection between backache and the skin may appear to be, the fact remains that anything that improves the functions of the latter will inevitably render us less susceptible to the former.

If, therefore, we accept the proposition that frequent hot baths are potentially harmful, it is a logical corollary that the natural alternative is to wash only in cool or cold water and, instead of the ritual morning hot bath, to have a cool or cold shower or sponge-down. The beneficial effects will be further enhanced if the body is dried vigorously with a coarse towel which will serve the double purpose of stimulating the circulation and generating a warm, glowing reaction.

The sum total of this and other recommendations which we have made will mean the adoption of a way of life in which potentially destructive habits are replaced by a constructive regimen: a simple, wholesome diet which provides the essential nutrients needed to build and maintain strong, healthy tissues; physical activity to oxygenate the blood, strengthen the heart, and activate the 'muscle-pump'; rest and relaxation to relieve stress and tension and recharge the body's batteries.

I commend to the reader what I hope he or she will recognize not only as a logical solution to the problem of backache but also as the best possible insurance against the many other organic and systemic illnesses and breakdowns which bedevil so many of us today.

Summary of Treatment

1. Pain Relief
Chapter 8, pages 70–81. Carry out whatever measures are appropriate and practicable, depending upon the nature, severity, and duration of the symptoms and the patient's physical condition.

2. Tissue-cleaning Regime
Chapter 9, pages 82–96, and Appendix A, pages 111–116. It is *essential* that this part of the treatment programme is carried out conscientiously in order to

clear the tissues of weakening and debilitating toxic residues and allow the body's innate healing and repair facilities to operate as speedily and efficiently as possible, and rebuild the damaged spinal tendons and ligaments.

3. Strengthening and Mobilizing Procedures

Chapter 10, pages 97–102, and Appendix C, pages 120–124. Once the painful symptoms have been relieved it is necessary to coax back into full mobility joints and supporting tissues which have stiffened and weakened due to enforced inactivity. A programme of graduated activities is necessary to break down adhesions and restore suppleness and elasticity to the muscles, tendons, and cartilages.

4. Avoiding a Recurrence.

Chapter 11, pages 103–109. Awareness of the types of everyday activities which put the spine at risk provides the best possible assurance of continuing immunity from backache as we grow older.

Appendix A

The cleansing regime

The 'spring-cleaning' regime can be carried out at any time of the year, but it is advisable, whenever possible, to choose a period when for a few days at least, and preferably a week, it is possible to rest as much as possible and be relatively free from social and occupational commitments.

For many people this is likely to mean starting treatment on a Friday so that the initial and more restrictive phase of the schedule is undertaken at a week-end, but others may be able to take a few days' holiday. The busy housewife or the mother of young children may be able to enlist the help of her spouse or another relative to relieve her of some of the more pressing demands on her time and energies.

Differing circumstances may, of course, necessitate making minor adjustments to the sequence and timing of meals, exercise sessions, etc., but provided that the prescribed treatments are fitted into the daily schedule minor changes are quite permissible. For example, the midday and evening meals may be interchanged, but no significant alterations in quantities or components should be made, and the outdoor exercise may be taken at any convenient time during the day or evening.

The relaxation and deep-breathing sessions should be introduced into the programme as soon as practicable, and the same applies to the progressive remedial exercises (see appendix B, page 117) and the daily outdoor exercise sessions.

With these reservations in mind, a start should be made as follows:

First Three Days

1. Before rising:
Lie on back, hands resting lightly on the lower abdomen, and breathe in slowly and deeply, allowing the chest and abdomen to rise and expand. Hold for two or three seconds then exhale. Repeat 12 times.

2. On rising:
Each morning take a tumbler of one of the proprietary mineral waters, such as Malvern, Evian, Perrier, etc., sipping it slowly. If mineral water is not obtainable, dissolve a level teaspoon of Epsom salts or Glauber's salts in a tumbler of warm water.

3. Breakfast:
Up to 300g (12 oz) of any *one* kind of fresh fruit, such as apples, oranges, pears, grapes, or grapefruit, but *not* bananas, and half a tumbler of freshly pressed or bottled unsweetened fruit juice diluted with an equal quantity of water.

4. Gentle walk:
If practicable, combined with deep breathing.

5. Midday meal:
As for breakfast, or a bowl of vegetable soup may be taken instead of dilute fruit juice if preferred (see recipe in Appendix C, page 120).

6. Evening meal:
As midday.

7. During evening:
Relaxation session (see Chapter 8, page 75). Retire early in a warm but well-ventilated bedroom. If a window cannot be partially opened, the door should be left ajar.

Notes:
Only *one* type of fruit may be taken at each meal. Water or dilute fruit juice may be drunk at any time, but *only* when needed to satisfy thirst. No other foods or beverages of any kind are permitted.

Those who are overweight may with advantage extend this initial stage of the cleansing regime to four or five days if circumstances permit.

Next Four Days

1. Before rising:
Deep breathing.

2. On rising:
Take the juice of an orange or half a lemon in a large

glass of water, sweetened if desired with a teaspoon of honey, but no other sweetener is permitted.

3. Breakfast:
Fruit only as on previous days.

4. Outdoor exercise:
And deep breathing if practicable.

5. Midday meal:
As on previous days.

6. Evening meal:
Raw salad consisting of any available items such as lettuce, tomato, watercress, diced or sliced carrot or apple with any two steamed green or root vegetables except potatoes.

7. During evening:
Relaxation session and retire early.

Notes:
During this initial phase of the treatment the eliminative organs are likely to be increasingly active as accumulated toxic residues are cleared from the tissues, giving rise to such symptoms as headache, general malaise, furred tongue, etc. This should not cause concern since it is indicative that the purpose of the cleansing regime is being effected. The symptoms should abate in the course of a few days during which time it is desirable to rest as much as possible. On no account should aspirin or any other medicament be taken.

8th to 14th Days
Continue as for preceding days except:

1. Breakfast:
The same quantity of fresh fruit but mixed varieties may be taken if preferred.

2. Midday meal:
Raw salad as previous evening meal with vegetables and one or two slices of wholewheat bread or toast or crispbread spread thinly with low-fat margarine.

3. Evening meal:
Vegetable soup, followed by two or three steamed vegetables, except potatoes, 50g (2oz) grated cheese or an egg — poached or scrambled — and one or two items of fresh fruit.

15th to 21st Days
As for preceding days except:

1. Midday meal:
Large mixed salad with toast or crispbread or a baked jacket potato.

2. Evening meal:
Two or three steamed vegetables with a little lean meat or fish, or an egg or cheese dish. Fresh fruit salad, or soaked or stewed dried fruit, sweetened if desired with a little honey, or a baked apple.

Notes:
The natural roughage in the diet, combined with outdoor exercise where possible and the remedial exercises, should ensure normal digestive and bowel

function provided that over-eating has been avoided and the food has been eaten slowly and masticated thoroughly. Any slight bowel sluggishness which may be experienced need cause no anxiety since peristaltic rhythm will soon be re-established.

Once the cleansing programme has been completed it is essential that the body's innate capacity for self-healing and reconstruction be allowed to operate at maximum efficiency. It *must*, therefore, be provided with the best quality nutritional materials, and every effort should be made to establish dietary habits which provide all the minerals, vitamins, and other essentials in their natural forms and combinations.

The specimen menus in Appendix C on page 120 exemplify a balanced dietary plan based on whole foods which will serve as a blue-print for future use. Within the scope of the 20:20:60 formula, considerable variety and interest can be sustained, and because unprocessed staple foods take the place of expensive denatured and chemicalized commercial products better health for the whole family should be achieved without the penalty of increased house-keeping costs.

Appendix B

Remedial exercises

The following exercises should be introduced progressively, repeating each movement up to six times as physical capacity permits, the aim being *gradually* to stretch thickened and contracted tendons, reduce fibrous adhesions and restore mobility to joints which have suffered as a result of strain or injury.

Movements should be carried only to the point where pain becomes manifest, and no attempt should be made to enforce additional mobility.

The ultimate objective is to practise the full programme at least once daily, but preferably twice — on rising and before retiring, or at any other convenient times.

1. Stand or sit erect with head held high and hands pressing lightly on the abdomen with finger-tips touching and thumbs just under the lower-rib margins. Breathe out slowly and deeply through the nose, feeling the ribs rising and the abdomen protruding slightly as the diaphragm contracts. Breathe out

slowly, allowing the ribs to lower and pulling in the abdomen strongly. Relax for a few seconds and repeat.

2. Same starting position: keeping the shoulders still, turn the head as far as possible to the right, back to the front, then to the left. Relax and repeat.

3. Same position: lower the chin onto the chest, then raise it as high as possible. Relax and repeat.

4. Same position: move the head so that the nose rotates in as wide a circle as possible — up, right, down, left. Rest and repeat in the reverse direction.

Note:
The range of movement in exercises 2, 3, and 4 is likely to be limited at first and special care should be taken to avoid undue strain. Crackling and creaking noises may be heard, but they need cause no concern and they should diminish gradually and eventually cease as joint mobility improves.

5. Lying on the back, with arms at sides, flex one hip and draw the knee towards the chest as far as possible, then return slowly to starting position and repeat with the other leg. Relax for a few seconds and repeat.

6. Same position: flex both hips simultaneously, draw the knees towards the chest, then return slowly to starting position. Relax and repeat.

7. Kneel down, with thighs vertical and hands on floor directly under shoulders, flex the knees slowly until the buttocks rest on the heels, then lower the forehead to the floor. Return slowly to starting position, rest and repeat.

8. Repeat first part of exercise 5, then with buttocks resting on the heels, rotate the shoulders to the right and reach with the *left* hand towards the *right* hip. Return slowly to starting position and repeat in opposite direction. Rest and repeat.

9. Lying on the back with arms fully extended to the sides, fully flex the hips and knees then, keeping the shoulders flat on the floor, swing the flexed legs as far as possible to the right. Return slowly to starting position, rest and repeat in opposite direction.

Special note:
In some lesions of the lower spine acute pain is localized on one side, radiating from the hip down the sciatic nerve into the thigh and leg. In these cases, movements *towards* the affected side will increase pressure on the nerve and may evoke severe pain and should therefore be avoided, whereas flexion or turning in the opposite direction will decompress the nerve and relieve the pain, and so may be attempted with due caution.

Appendix C

Wholefood guidelines and menus

The basic rules which need to be observed in establishing a wholefood dietary regime are simple:

1. Avoid as far as possible all refined starches and sugars — e.g. white flour, white bread, white sugar, cakes, pastries, sweetened breakfast cereals, and white rice and pastas, as well as tinned and packeted 'convenience foods' which have been precooked and 'fortified' with synthetic vitamins and minerals, and which contain many dubious chemicals in the form of flavourings, colourings, preservatives, texturizers, extenders, etc. Study the contents panel on the label!

2. Avoid fried and other very fatty foods, highly spiced and flavoured dishes as well as salt and other condiments. Use only in strict moderation animal fats in the form of meat, butter, cheese, and whole milk. Unsaturated fats in the form of vegetable oils, soft margarines, nuts, etc. should be used in preference to animal derivatives.

3. Choose fresh fruit and vegetables instead of tinned and precooked products. Do not store them longer than necessary and cook them as quickly as possible in the minimum of water. Use the latter as stock or to make soups or casseroles. When possible, scrub root vegetables and fruits but do not peel them unnecessarily.

4. Use only wholegrain cereals in the form of wholewheat flour, 100 per cent wholemeal bread, crispbread, muesli, brown rice, and wholemeal pastas, but keep strictly to the 20 per cent daily ration.

Specimen Menus

Breakfast:
- Two or three items of fresh fruit — e.g. an apple, orange, some grapes, banana, pear, ½ grapefruit, with ¼ pt natural yogurt.
- Stewed fresh fruit (sweetened with a little honey if desired), or soaked or stewed dried fruit sprinkled with a dessertspoon of wheatgerm.
- Muesli (see recipe on page 123).
- One or two slices of wholewheat toast with a poached or scrambled egg or 50g (2oz) cottage cheese.
- Not more than twice weekly — a wholegrain breakfast cereal moistened with two or three dessertspoons of skimmed milk, sweetened if desired with a little honey.

Midday:
- A small mixed salad consisting of several items in season — e.g. lettuce, celery, tomato, watercress,

cucumber, and sliced or diced raw carrot or
cooked beetroot — with one slice of wholemeal
bread or crispbread spread thinly with low-fat
margarine and yeast extract or peanut butter, if
desired.
- Two or three steamed root or green vegetables
  with 50g (2oz) of lean meat or fish, or a vegetarian savoury.
- On those days when a fruit breakfast has been
  taken, two or three slices of wholemeal bread, or
  toast, or crispbread with a poached or scrambled
  egg, or 50g (2oz) cheese, and an apple, pear, or
  banana.

Evening:
- A mixed vegetable casserole sprinkled with 50g
  (2oz) grated cheese per person, followed by fresh
  fruit salad and ¼ pt natural yogurt.
- A large mixed salad (see recipe on page 124) with
  two slices of wholemeal bread, toast or crispbread
  spread with low-fat margarine and honey, yeast
  extract, or peanut butter, followed by stewed or
  soaked dried fruit (e.g. prunes, apricots, figs,
  raisins, or sultanas) sprinkled with a dessertspoon
  of wheatgerm.
- Two or three steamed green or root vegetables
  with 50g (2oz) of lean meat or fish, or an
  omelette, or a vegetarian savoury, followed by
  fresh fruit or sliced banana and natural yogurt.

Notes:
1. Ensure that some fresh fruit and a salad is
   included in each day's menu.
2. Vegetables and fruit should not be chopped finely

or grated as this causes maximum destruction of vitamins. Instead, they should be diced or sliced and then served immediately. Leaves of lettuce and other green vegetables, when served raw, should be served whole or torn into pieces.

3. Proprietary salad dressings, salt, pickles, and other condiments should not be added to food either during preparation or at table. If desired, salads may be lightly dressed with natural yogurt or a dessertspoon of vegetable oil (e.g. olive, sunflower, or corn) mixed with a teaspoon of lemon juice. A little celery salt may be used to season vegetables if desired.

4. Drinks should consist mainly of water, or dilute fresh fruit or vegetable juice, or half a teaspoon of yeast extract in a tumbler of water. A cup of unsweetened tea or decaffeinated coffee may be taken occasionally if desired.

Recipes

Vegetable Soup
Prepare approximately 2 kg (4½lb) of any vegetables — e.g. carrots, cabbage, peas, beans, celery, onions, spinach, etc. — diced or sliced as necessary, cover with 1¼ litres (2 pt) boiling water and simmer for one hour. Strain and flavour with yeast extract, but do not add salt or other condiments.

Muesli
2 or 3 heaped dessertspoons of coarse oatmeal or muesli cereal base.
1 heaped dessertspoon washed raisins, or sultanas, or chopped dates.

2 heaped dessertspoons grated nuts — e.g. peanuts, hazels, cashews, etc.

½ medium apple.

½ ripe banana.

1 dessertspoon honey (optional).

4 dessertspoons warm water, or half skimmed milk and water.

Mix the dried fruit into the cereal, melt the honey (if desired) in the warm water, pour over and leave to soak for one hour or overnight.

Before serving, add the finely chopped apple, sprinkle over the grated nuts and decorate with banana slices.

A little more milk or water may be added if desired.

Mixed Salad

Any salad vegetables in season — e.g. lettuce, tomato, celery, carrot, celeriac, cucumber, watercress, beetroot (raw or cooked but no vinegar). 1 dessertspoon washed dried fruit — e.g. raisins, sultanas, dates.

50g (2oz) cheese.

50g (2oz) nuts.

½ medium apple.

½ ripe banana.

Tear the lettuce or other green vegetables into pieces and line a large plate, then decorate with sliced tomato, cucumber, diced carrot, etc. Sprinkle over the dried fruit and the diced apple, followed by the grated cheese and grated nuts, and finally decorate with banana slices.

Index